FORGET THE JOB,
NAIL THE INTERVIEW!

A Humorous Look at the Triumphs and Pitfalls of the Job Interview

Matt Alexander, MBA

This book is specially dedicated to all those people who believed in me, but
only made possible by those who didn't.

Copyright 2009

Author's Note

Putting all of this together was a trip down memory lane for me. I have woven a number of personal stories into the fabric of the text. Writing this way makes it easy to move from topic to topic, but I have dutifully tried to organize the chapters to be of the most benefit to my reader. For the most part, the story builds to a crescendo, starting with getting the invitation to interview, preparing in a variety of ways, and finally making your big appearance and presentation. We conclude with some follow up etiquette, and an interesting story that demonstrates that every action you take in life is actually part of an interview.

I have omitted specific names to protect both the innocent and the guilty, but mostly myself. All of the stories are true so if you see yourself somewhere, it could be you.

Matt Alexander

The Goal of our Adventure

In developing the title for this work, I took a cue from what any good self help coach will tell you. When you set goals, make them measurable, reasonable and attainable. The overall goal of my reader is to get a new job, but setting that as a goal can be too overwhelming. Thus, we break it down to one of several brass rings for which we are reaching, something reasonable, attainable and measurable, that is- nail the interview.

Table of Contents

Preface		7
1.	How Important is This Thing Anyway?	11
2.	What An Opportunity!	16
3.	No Really, I can Do This	20
4.	Moving Beyond the Fear of Rejection	24
5.	Time For Plan B	29
6.	A Plan Kept Close To The Vest	33
7.	Glad That One Got Away!	36
8.	Hell No! I Won't Go!	44
9.	The Sure Thing	47
10.	How's This Group Gonna Work?	53
11.	One On One	62
12.	Meet the Competition	69
13.	What Would You Like to Know?	73
14.	You Tell Us	76
15.	We'd Also Like to Know (2nd Tier)	83
16.	A Little Thoughtfulness Now (3rd Tier)	91
17.	Excuse me?!	102
18.	Do Like This	108
19.	The Flip Side of Questions	113
20.	The All Important Question of $$$	120
21.	Showing Up, and Looking Good	126
22.	Um, Is This My Floor?	134
23.	Travel Light	138

24.	Into the Fire	141
25.	Play Nice	149
26.	Follow up	153
27.	And Now We Wait	159
Epilogue		163

Preface

When I originally thought of writing down these tidbits of wisdom for posterity, I had no idea of how the local, national and even global economy would be changing as it headed toward recession, and how valuable this information might be for increasing numbers of people who have been, or will be laid off from their jobs, not to mention the steady stream of freshly minted college graduates. I didn't even know how much I would need them myself.

My timing has always been impeccable. I graduated from college, grad school and the Navy during recessions. The times were tough, but somehow I always found a soft spot to land on.

There are many, many books available that discuss the job search in general, and many more that cover such areas as resumes, networking and career counseling. In this book, I am concentrating solely on the interview portion of the job search and its related soul searching and confidence building. More specifically, how to prepare, what will happen during the interview and how to react both during and after your big show. Realizing that this whole process can be one of the most stressful activities you will ever engage in, I have tried, by relating a number of true life stories, to lighten the tone, yet provide vitally important information.

Over the past twenty five years or so I've almost always been employed. There has never been any hesitancy on my part to tackle difficult jobs, some involving hard physical labor or unpleasant tasks, others requiring relentless pursuit of a specified goal, regardless of the burden of the commitment. Through this, I have had several different jobs. It's funny how you make all sorts of plans for your future, but as time goes by you make changes in the plan, or changes are made for you. I started with career goals, but changed my mind about the career along the way. Several times.

As a kid I wanted to be all the normal things- cowboy, fireman, and soldier. That changed to spy, oceanographer and adventurer. By the time I got out of high school I had visions of medical school in my mind. Somehow that changed to business school. In actuality I ended up graduating from college with a very valuable degree in Anthropology. You laugh, but the skills I learned there, and not in eighth grade English class, are what have enabled me to put these words together into sentences.

So, my "career" path is certainly not a straight line. Most recently, I have set a personal record of successfully, and stressfully, progressing through three totally different jobs in a single year. Considering that the statistics say a job search can take up to eight months and often much longer for that *just right* job, I think that's pretty damn good. Maybe good isn't quite the word for it since it would have been nice to stay in at least one of those jobs for quite a bit longer, but I do think it's quite an accomplishment to get three jobs in one year. Take note, however, I do not recommend that as a career goal to anyone.

In business school we looked at lots of charts and graphs, and people's careers can be compared in some ways to those lines. Some have straight, flat lines. Take a job, stay for twenty years and never advance. Some have rising lines. Get that job and smoothly ride that gravy train up through the ranks. Some charts show a declining path, with someone taking a job, failing, and dropping out of the work force.

More common I would think are the jagged line paths, where people take a job and have ups and downs with it. They may switch positions within a company, or switch between companies in an industry, sometimes being higher or lower on the totem pole. My experience however is a series of disconnected jagged lines, switching positions, switching companies, switching industries. Several total makeovers. It hasn't always been easy, or enjoyable, but I have broadened my horizons. And, I've had many, many, many opportunities to go on interviews.

Not everything here has been gleaned from my experience as an interviewee. I've also been in the position of conducting interviews, so that perspective is represented as well. I think the reader can benefit from both.

Over the years, as I pursued my own employment adventure, I've read several books on the subject of "get a job," and some of the information presented here will sound like I have recounted it from standard textbook stuff. However, what I've learned is that nothing can prepare you for something better than experience and I will try to provide guidance to any and all who care to listen to a battle hardened front line interviewer who has no qualification for giving advice other than that personal experience.

It's kind of what a mathematician might call faulty logic. To have a good interview you need interviewing experience. Unfortunately, on the job training in this arena has major pitfalls. If you screw up the interview, you don't get the job. You only get one shot. So, to get the experience, you must fail miserably, and thus learn, along the way.

Hopefully this little book will be helpful in giving you some real insight into actual interviewing scenarios. Sure, you could take a class, or get a bunch of friends together for a brainstorming session and practice drills, but if the teacher or the friends haven't been there, some of this stuff is beyond your wildest imagination. When you take some time, read the stories, and share a laugh, you'll be a little better equipped to prepare, relax and...**nail the interview!**

Chapter 1
How Important is This Thing Anyway?

At the time it seemed like a pretty big deal, but I had no idea just how important this event would be in my future. I was in graduate school working on a fancy degree, and looking for my first job. The university career center had set up an interview day for the students. Twenty or so companies were coming to interview candidates for spectacular career opportunities.

There was a list of the companies coming and you had to sign up in advance to meet with their representatives. Each company had certain times and a private office to use. The one thing the career center had neglected to do was give anyone any clues as to how to ensure that we handled ourselves professionally in these interviews. No sample questions to ponder. No tips for how to dress to impress. There was no social skills advice. Basically, we were on our own. I guess the Career Center felt that graduates of a prestigious private university's master's level program had already been to charm school and were loaded with common sense. I think I was sick the day of the charm school lecture.

The name of the company escapes me these many years later, but I remember several other things about that first interview very well. Sensory perceptions remain about the room, the seating arrangement, the discomfort and the nervousness. And most of all, I remember that it was a disaster. That first question, after the formalities of introductions and extending a clammy hand, was a defining moment in my life. It wasn't until many years later that I would realize this however.

"So, tell me a little about yourself," were his fateful words. I had two college degrees from pretty good schools, I'd done some world traveling and I had held several jobs, but under the pressure cooker environment of the interview, my best response was "what would you like to know?" I don't remember anything after that, except that it was bad.

What did I learn from that? The biggest lesson was one I should have learned in the Boy Scouts, or as a graduate student, or in any number of other life circumstances. I should have been prepared. Knowing what you are talking about, or at least presenting that image, is the key to successful public speaking, whether in front of a crowd of thousands or just one other person.

Over the years I've interviewed for many jobs. Sometimes you can interview well but not get the job, but it's pretty rare that you interview poorly and do get the job. Interviews for every job I thought I wanted haven't been forthcoming, and being chosen as "the one" after every interview I was invited to wasn't always the outcome, but I like to tell myself that given my experience, I have become a professional interviewer.

Of course the desired result is that we get the job in the end, but to get to the finish line, we have to punch the many tickets along the way. The interview is a critical ticket punch and I'd put myself up against anyone in conducting an excellent interview. Even if I have no qualifications for the job opening, I can do one heck of an interview!

In defense of this claim, I will unabashedly tell you about an incident that I experienced and in hindsight is quite hilarious. At least my shrink thought so when I told him.

On several occasions I applied for a position with a state government agency located near my home. The job was for some kind of computer marketing analyst. The agency would be good to work for, the pay was good, and the commute would be timed in single digit numbers. It sounded interesting and I thought, "what the hell, I can do that work even if I don't have the exact qualifications they are looking for." Guess what? After three or four applications, I never heard back.

Another position with this agency later presented itself and for this I was perfectly well qualified, overqualified even. I had the skills, the education and the experience. They couldn't deny me. When I got the call from so and so saying the agency wanted me to come in for an interview, I thought, "great, I'll be facilities manager there and it will be really close to home."

I had forgotten all about the computer marketing analyst job. But I remembered when I started to do some homework in preparing for the interview. It's a good idea to get the names of the folks you will be talking to in advance. That way you can do some internet searching to find out a little bit about them. You might be able to drop a surprise compliment on them when you meet.

I had been told who I'd be meeting with but according to the agency website, none of those names were of people who worked in facilities. My nerves were steadied by telling myself that this was going to be a group interview with a wide representation of departments. Facilities managers work with all the departments to keep everyone happy, right? But it wasn't a wide representation of departments. Not in the broadest sense anyway. All of these people had something to do with Information Technology. Doubt entered my mind, but I wasn't sure.

The first question posed to me at the interview confirmed my worst suspicions. I was there for the computer job! Oh my, I'd prepared myself for the facilities job with good answers and good questions, but now I had to really think on my feet. Thoughts were racing through my head- what job was I here for, what was the job description and do I meet the requirements for that computer thing? How the heck am I gonna fake my way through this without looking like a total idiot!

I still don't know the answer to the last one, but somehow I did it. The other questions don't matter because, yeah, you guessed it, I didn't get the job. Probably wouldn't have liked it anyway. I spent an hour talking to nine people about a job I couldn't even remember and somehow

I answered their questions with some degree of intelligence.

I never got the sense that they were as lost as I was, or that they realized I was lost. I must know a little about this interviewing business. You might be as good as me and fake your way through it, but my best advice is go into the interview knowing what job you are talking about.

- **A good interview will bring you one step closer to the goal.**
- **A bad interview will likely eliminate you from the competition.**
- **Be prepared.**
- **Know what you are talking about.**

Chapter 2
What An Opportunity!

If you've gotten to the point of going on an interview, you probably have already done the soul searching involved in deciding what you want to do when you grow up. No? That's ok. If you applied for a job, and are headed to an interview, at least you've convinced someone that you might be qualified for the work involved.

There are three types of jobs out there- the one's we'd like to do, the one's we can do, and the one's we don't want to do. I've always heard that if you do what you like, then you'll never work a day in your life.

Never say never. That dream job is a possibility. Depending on where you are in your career or life, you may be ready for that job. Let's look at the facts. First, that dream job has to exist, or you have to create it. It may actually be out there just waiting for you, but you have to know how to find it. Let me just say here that there are many places to look, and other publications go into quite a bit of detail in this regard so I will keep my own comments very brief. The best thing I can tell you is that an offer for a good job is very unlikely to come to you out of the blue while you sit on the sofa watching TV and eating potato chips, or anything else for that matter. You must look.

Second, you have to be able to physically and mentally do the work involved. Here are a couple of examples of what

I mean. I always wanted to be a super fast downhill ski racer. Olympic gold medal hanging on my neck, you know? It looks so cool on TV to be hurtling down the mountainside at eighty or ninety miles an hour, all tucked up like a ball blasting through the wind and fighting every second to stay on your feet. The only thing holding me back is that as a recreational skier I learned that I was afraid to go too fast. Most beginners can tell you that falling down hurts, and crashing at ninety miles an hour would hurt a lot.

Most men would say that they have had visions of being a professional athlete. Seems like fun. Lots of money. Considerable fame. So why not? In my case, it's because I'm too old, overweight and uncoordinated.

And finally, although this is certainly not the end of a list of things I'm not qualified to do, I always wanted to be a doctor. You know, a brain surgeon. Lots of money. Live the good life. It didn't occur to me until my freshman year in college that I didn't care too much for studying either math or science.

So, that perfect job is great, but you have to have the skills, abilities, education, experience and personality to be successful. Even then you'll find some aspect of that "dream" job that's more nightmare than dream. So let's close up the daydreams and focus a little more on the real world.

Sometimes when you apply for a job, you are responding to a specific posting you saw somewhere which described some organization's need to fill a certain job requiring a certain skill set and experience and education and all of that. You might have looked in the newspaper or Yahoo-hotjobs, or craigslist or any number of other such sources.

On the other hand, professional job hunters (as opposed to professional interviewers like me) will tell you that the best way to find a job is to tap into the unseen job market. You do this by networking. I always enjoyed reading the job hunter's books. Sounds so easy. Just join a lot of professional organizations and be an active member. You meet a lot of people and have an opportunity to tell them all about your abilities. You can also talk to people in the field you are interested in to get their inputs. These are great resources and if you can take advantage of them that is great.

I will say that doing a job search this way can lead you down some funny paths. In many cases, finding a job through networking means talking to people about jobs that don't really exist. You may have been granted an interview just to talk in general about the industry or business. The interviewer might just be thinking about hiring someone down the road a few days, months or years

Going into this kind of interview, you need to be prepared for frustration on your part, and to convince someone that they should create an opening for you. You'd better be good, and the best way to put that best foot forward is to know what kind of job you'd like and tell them to create it.

Many years ago I made an appointment to meet with a man who was a member of my church. He had known my wife's parents for many, many years. He was also very big in the business community as the former mayor of the city I live in, and the president of the largest local bank.

At the time, he was retired from all of this and was perhaps losing some of his connections and clout, but he was still an excellent resource. We talked a great deal about his background, and mine, and what I'd like to do and what he thought I would be qualified for.

Going into this meeting I knew he couldn't actually find me a job, or make me a job. What I was looking for was his rolodex. I mean, I was hoping he would give me the names of some of his connections to talk with. And that did happen. From there I got two more "informational" interviews. Unfortunately, neither of them was instrumental in my finding a new job.

- **You need some clear idea as to what kind of job you want.**
- **Talk to people about where you might find such a job.**
- **Know what is, and isn't possible. Aim high, but be real.**

Chapter 3
No Really, I Can Do This

I call myself a generalist, or a big picture person, because I can do a lot of things a little bit, but nothing exceptionally well. I just don't have the detail orientation, or the ability to sit still long enough. Career wise, that can lead to moving around from job to job, never getting the finer points of doing any particular thing. It can also put you into the enviable position of being able to be a manager anywhere. Provided that the people hiring that manager appreciate the executive skills you've developed.

There was a time when it seemed like all the big companies were getting new CEOs. They never had any experience in that particular industry; they just knew business and how to run a company. Now college degrees are so specialized, and work tasks are so minutely defined, that there is little room for someone like me who is just good at thinking and problem solving and making things work better.

Good job descriptions are hard to write, so often they are poorly done. Incomplete mostly, but sometimes just plain old deceptive. Some are so broad based that almost anyone who is breathing would qualify, and others are so detailed and specific that there can surely only be one superhuman person who is capable of filling the post. And sometimes they are written one way, but what is really called for is something very different. I myself have written job descriptions so specific that only that one person who I have pre-selected has even a snowball's chance of qualifying for. Some specific skill or knowledge of some obscure software package is demanded.

When you are on the hiring side of the desk, this is a clever tactic for getting what you want, and not unreasonable. But from the applicant side of the desk, it can be very frustrating. "I can learn that," you say. Or, "how specialized can this be?" I'll just remind you here of my over dramatized analogy of having a degree in left hand screw turning when a degree in right hand screw turning is required, and the two are absolutely not interchangeable.

How many times have you seen a job that you would like to do, but maybe don't have the strongest qualifications for? You know you could learn it, or go right in and do it, if only someone would give you a chance. If you are really lucky, your resume might catch the eye of someone who is a visionary thinker, or can at least think enough outside the box to realize that you might be a good fit. You might find a person who either can or will take off the tunnel vision goggles, see that you are intelligent, and take you for a test drive.

You know you're qualified, if only they'd give you a chance. But it's not you. They only see the gaps in your résumé and not what's written between the lines, have someone else in mind, or have a quota to fill.

Want to be a travel agent? Well sure, you have traveled, and you enjoy traveling, and you can learn the fool out of anything someone puts in front of you, but there are a hundred people in line ahead of you with a degree in travel agency management who also know sixteen different software systems specially designed for the travel business. Too bad. Rejected.

I never applied for anything I really didn't think I was qualified for, or at least capable of. The difference between the two is that in the first you already know how to do something, and have proven it, while in the second you are confident you could do it with training. That opens a lot of possibilities, but remember that in the mind of the recruiter, they want the strongest candidate, and that's usually going to be the one who is best qualified.

At some point I began to realize that with a degree in Anthropology, I could indeed think, and write, analyze and interpret, be creative and learn. But that isn't necessarily what employers are looking for. They are often looking for someone who will come in on the first day and know all the technical details of the work to be done. No time for training.

Maybe, in spite of all this, you can actually convince someone to interview you for a job you might be qualified for. There is no shame in not getting an interview for every job you apply for. Nor in not getting every job you interview for. Each interview is a learning experience exposing you to more questions, more practice, and helping you nail down the answers to questions. The best thing, however, is that it makes you know who you are and what

you've done so you can relate that to others very naturally without seeming stiff or like you are reciting a canned answer. Practice makes perfect.
- **No harm in asking for help**
- **Always do your best**
- **Don't fear the unknown**
- **Don't worry about failure**

Chapter 4
Moving Beyond the Fear of Rejection

Initially I stated that I was a professional interviewer, which by supposition means that I have been on a lot of interviews. If you look at my professional history, I have had a number of jobs, but not enough to automatically conclude that I have been on a lot of interviews.

My dad retired when he was 70 years old after he had worked for the same company for 42 years. How many times have you heard about days gone by when someone would get a gold watch when they retired after twenty years with the company? That's pretty rare today. People just don't stay put that long.

Some attribute that to needing to be mobile to advance. Some think that it's a matter of a lack of loyalty on the part of the employees. There is a good bit of evidence to show that employers don't have a whole lot of loyalty to their employees either though. Ever heard of someone being fired just before they have their twenty years in and are eligible for a pension? Ever seen an older, more experienced worker lose their job only to have some young person, who doesn't cost as much, replace them? Sure you have. It's not that uncommon.

I've read that people these days not only have multiple jobs during their lifetime, but they also have multiple careers. That is the demographic into which I fit.

But I digress. The point I was making is that I've been on interviews for jobs I didn't get. I'd have to think about it pretty carefully, but I don't think it would be untrue for me to say that I have been on more interviews for jobs I didn't get than for jobs I did get. So maybe I'm not such a good interviewer you say. Not so fast.

I've known people who have gotten every job they ever applied for. At least that's what they say. Not that I would doubt their veracity, but it just seems to me that such perfection in the pursuit of employment would be a little difficult. Maybe they just haven't had as many opportunities to look for work as I have. Maybe they have only had one job in their career.

In my own experience, there are going to be situations, and many of them, where you don't get the job. Sometimes that may even be because you aren't qualified for the position. But there are a few other reasons why you might come up short on the selection committee's list.

Your attire, appearance, timeliness, connections, race, sex, experience, personality, and other uncontrollable factors can, and do, all play a role. While the concept of political correctness is well entrenched in business today, and the laws of the land regarding discrimination are being strengthened, they are pretenders to the throne when it comes to the power of human nature. Hiring professionals will always talk the talk, but sometimes they just can't walk the walk, and prejudice and bias sneak into the equation.

Sometimes they just don't hire you, for what seem like dark and mysterious reasons. The unspoken and unacknowledged reasons that contrary to the law or public assertion really do exist. I'm a middle aged white guy at this point and have felt the impact of affirmative action as well as prejudice and favoritism. Not being an activist, I've always just shook my head and chalked it up to reality, but it still makes me, well, frustrated sometimes. Discrimination and reverse discrimination work the same way, and are equally unfair and painful. They don't always seem as apparent however.

I know that I have been interviewed on occasion to fill a quota for interviewees. Token white. Token male. Token old person. A white guy applying for a job in the office of cultural diversity at a university doesn't really have a chance. Nor does a man applying for a position in the area of Women's Studies. And some might even argue that why would they even want to. Could be, plain and simple, that they are really interested in that area of endeavor.

I interviewed for a job as an accountant in an office that worked with foreign affairs. With an MBA, I can do some accounting, I like to travel, and that anthropology degree taught me a good bit about foreign culture. When I left the interview there was some nonverbal chit chat between the interviewers and the administrative assistant leading me away which I definitely interpreted as "this guy is a super candidate." So, I was a little surprised when I got a call saying that I didn't get the job, but that I was smart and handsome and wouldn't have a problem finding a good job. The smart part I'm reasonably confident about. The handsome part I can probably argue with in some ways, but what the hell, what does that have to do with anything anyway? Just a little subtle form of discrimination.

It turns out that the big boss wanted someone who was actually a foreigner to have the job. Someone who was also a friend of the big boss. No matter that she wasn't an accountant. How many of these stories can I tell? How high can you count?

One of my favorites though was when I was interviewing to be a small business consultant. I went to the interview well prepared, and answered a slew of questions all to the satisfaction of my inquisitors. As I left they all seemed to be very upbeat about my candidacy. Several days later I got a call from the chairman of the selection committee and he asked one further question, "Can you think of anything else that you didn't say at your interview that would make me lean toward you in our choice?" He seemed almost desperate for me to come up with some incredible new bit of information. I recounted a number of my strong points, but didn't really cover any new ground. He seemed satisfied, but then blew me away by saying that it was between me and another man. That's not surprising, but he went on to further say that the other man hadn't been interviewed yet because he'd been shot during a crime. And he wasn't the victim of the crime. He got the job. Hmmmmm?!

The one that always festered in my pride filled craw was the guy who beat me out of not just one job, but two! We had both applied for the same job, and he beat me out because I was looking for a higher salary than him. Several years later we both applied for the same job again, with another company. He beat me again, primarily because he had held the first job and had thus acquired some experience that gave him the edge.

- **There are many reasons why you might not be hired.**
- **If you trust in your abilities, don't be afraid to spread your wings.**
- **Be prepared to pick yourself up, dust yourself off, and try again!**

Chapter 5
Time for Plan B

Rejection can be very hard to deal with and may make your job search even more difficult. Everyone deals with that in their own way, some more successfully than others. Personally, I have a high threshold for pain tolerance, can easily walk away from less than noble vices and don't care for the alternatives to not working.

I knew a guy who worked in a factory for many years. He got hurt and was never able to go back to work. Not because his injury prevented him from working, but because of his reaction to the injury. He started drinking because of the pain, then decided he couldn't work, got bitter and drank more. Like I said, never did go back to work. In all my memories of this man, I cannot remember ever seeing him out of his TV watching chair, and that is where he died.

Some people will turn to self help books. Like some of you reading this book. My advice at least is based on my personal experiences as a rat in the race as opposed to other authors whose knowledge comes from the study of rat behavior from the vantage point of a cat. What color is your parachute? Considering the fact that I've just been tossed out of the airplane, I don't really care what color the damn thing is, I just want it to work. Maybe after I land safely I can think about what color to pack next time.
Television loves to tell stories of losers who became winners. They don't always measure losing very well. One

day I was watching one of the morning news stories and they were having a special guest- someone who had turned a pink slip during a bad economy into cotton candy. Turns out she had decided to go out on her own into the fashion industry after getting her third pink slip in fifteen years. Now she runs a multimillion dollar fashion accessory company.

I don't think three jobs in fifteen years is a big deal. Look at me; I've had three jobs in the past 15 months! Even though I left those three jobs for different reasons, that's the kind of thing that makes you start to think that maybe there is something wrong with you. After lengthy consultation with my shrink, I decided that it wasn't so much me per se, as me being in the wrong job. There we are back to the original question of what do I want to be when I grow up?

It can be very frustrating to be told that after earning two college degrees you are incapable of learning the skills needed to do a certain job. For instance, and this may be a little exaggerated, if you have a degree in turning screws to the right, you are totally unsuitable for a job that requires turning screws to the left. When hiring professionals are looking at the skill sets needed to perform a job they are trying to fill, they will often be totally focused on those specific skills. The box is very well defined, and they refuse or look beyond its four corners.

For many years I was determined that my record spoke for itself, and that I would, and could, make it on my own.

Just plain old stubborn I guess. Life would have been a lot easier, a lot earlier, if I'd listened to some sage advice which I am now passing on. You should listen.

There was this really good job advertised for someone to work as a special projects assistant to the Senior Vice President of Finance at a local organization, and I wanted it. Basically it was managing the finances and record keeping of one of the more exciting divisions within the company. The competition would be fierce for this and I knew I was going to have to make a face to face pitch to be selected. But, I had to get that face time first.

The Senior VP was a man I had met once before at a party. Sometimes meeting people at parties isn't very helpful because they may be enjoying themselves and not remember you later. But I remembered him. And I was close to some other people who knew him well both professionally and socially. A major effort was called for and I pulled out all the stops.

Someone told me to write directly to the man, and to tell him, "Joe sent me." Not Joe really, but to use their name. This time I did. I was amazed at the result of this action. A couple of days later the man's secretary called me to set up an interview. Man, this was gonna be great!

We had a long discussion about the job, and he seemed to take great interest in my background. I wasn't too surprised that someone else got the job; someone picked before my interview, but in fact was actually a tad heartened by the experience.

The rest of the story is that while I didn't get that job, the Senior VP did talk to my boss's boss and ask why my talents weren't being made better use of. I have no idea what the reply was, but I know the question, and the fact that I'd even had any contact with the Senior VP, seemed to surprise the heck out of the guy. He told me that one day when I went to talk to him about, well, about putting my skills to better use. Set in his opinions as much as he was, I never moved up and eventually moved on.

- **Don't let yourself get in your own way.**
- **Too much ego is not necessarily good.**
- **Don't be afraid to modify your methods.**

Chapter 6
A Plan Kept Close To The Vest

A lot of people don't talk about their interviewing history so it's hard to know who's looking, how often they look, and how successful their searches are. People usually don't want their current employer to know that they are looking for a new job. Makes for some awkward situations, no?

Say the boss finds out you are looking for a new job. The worst thing that can happen is that they say if you don't like it here then scram, and they escort you out of the building like a common criminal. Is that the worst thing though? Maybe not. Your boss may be the kind of person who decides they can make life hard on you until you get fed up and quit. That's ok if you've actually found that new job to go to; otherwise, it's worse than being fired. No unemployment when you voluntarily resign.

You could be one of the lucky ones I guess. If they find out you are looking for another job they'll call you into the corner office to entice you with more money or better perks or whatever it takes to make you stay. Lots of people threaten to quit and end up better off. My experience is that if you say you are going to quit, you better be prepared to do so.

After a number of years in my position at a major research university I told my boss he should be expecting a call from someone asking questions about me in regard to a new position for which I was applying. I had debated in my mind how do to deal with this- the potential employer wanted a reference from my current employer, but I didn't want the current employer to know I was looking. I had no choice. The job I was looking at was so much better than the one I had, and the odds were heavily stacked in my favor- purely because of my knowledge, skills and abilities. So I told him and he agreed to give a good reference. No attempt to stop me from leaving was ever made.

I would like to think, and have always done so, that he was happy for me in my opportunity to advance and that he had every confidence that I would do one hell of a job. Or maybe it was that he was glad to get rid of a lout like me and would do anything to be rid of me, even if it meant dumping me on some other poor unsuspecting soul. Hey, I've done that. But no, I am assured that he was happy for my opportunity to advance and did indeed provide an excellent reference.

It's very possible that in asking for a reference from your current employer, your would-be employer is screening out individuals who, for one reason or another, don't want their present boss to express an opinion. Maybe she won't give a good reference. Or perhaps, as discussed above, knowledge of your thought of departure might cause unpleasantness with your situation.

Thus, you may not always know that one of your coworkers is out interviewing for jobs until they come in one day and give their two week notice. Now, I hope that my reader won't get the idea that those unsuccessful interviews are really unsuccessful and that the fact that I've not gotten many of the positions I interviewed for is a bad thing. In my mind, each of these interviews was a learning experience. Besides, there are many reasons why you don't get a job you have interviewed for. And that so called failure may actually be a blessing in disguise.

- Lots of people keep their job search to themselves at their current place of employment.
- Sometimes you can't.
- Don't use interviews as a bargaining chip with your current boss.
- No interview is without value.

Chapter 7
Glad That One Got away!

There are some people who know from an early age exactly what they want to do, and do all the things it takes to get there. They know what company they want to work for, prepare with the proper education, interview with that company and get the job they want. I think they are the minority.

Others among us have such a broad based area of interest that they could do any number of things in a multitude of places, and thus have a great many possibilities to look at in terms of jobs to interview for. I think they may be a minority as well.

Most people, I believe, fall somewhere in between- they kind of know what they'd like to do, prepare for a number of things, and end up in something that interests them for the time being.

The first scenario leaves room for burnout, but otherwise provides a fairly stable and predictable career path. It is the latter two that leave room for a great deal of movement and the tendency to sometimes take a shotgun approach to job searching. That is, looking at a variety of things, all of which have some interest. This being the case, it is very likely that the job seeker will say to themselves, "that sounds interesting, I think I can do that, so I'll apply."

I am always amazed by people who seem to tread through a dung heap and come out smelling like roses. No real qualifications, but a sunny personality or incredible timing, or luck. They get one job that leads to another and another and another and before you know it they are president of the whole damn company. Or of their own spinoff. That of course doesn't happen to everyone, and that soul who willy-nilly said, "that sounds like fun," realizes, much to their dismay, that they have applied for something which they are pitifully unprepared for, or begin to understand far too late that it's not really what they want.

As discussed previously, there are many reasons why you might not be selected for a job. In some cases it may really be better to exercise your right of first refusal. I know, you really need a job, and this is the best one you've seen. And maybe under some circumstances you absolutely cannot refuse. But if you are on your toes, you will realize that just because a job is offered to you doesn't mean you have to take it. A list of compelling reasons to turn down a position might relieve some of the tension.

Let's start with an easy one- you decide, based on your interview, that you wouldn't like the job. It could be the people, the location, the environment or the work itself. I interviewed for a job in the mountainous region of a certain mid-Atlantic state once. It was a smaller company than I was really looking for, but would have been a stepping stone to something else. The only problem was, and this is just me, that waaaay up in the mountains, it seemed like isolation was the most abundant commodity. My family wouldn't have been happy there, so I said no to that one.

After I finished an interview with a company far from my home, I decided that before I hit the road I would stop by a real estate office to see what types of homes were available and at what price. I had learned from that out of town interview above that it is very important to get a feel for the community. Where would you live and what kind of housing options are available? What's the cost of living like? How are the schools? Are there social, cultural and recreational activities to suit your lifestyle? You don't want to take a job, move a thousand miles to a new community and suddenly find, to your horror, that you like the job, but not the community.

It was late, near closing time, but I went in and everyone was friendly. One of the agents engaged me in conversation as to what I was looking for and in a roundabout manner, why. When she found out I was there interviewing for the job, she let it be known that she was married to one of the principle officers and that the word on the street was that the selection committee was down to two applicants, me and another, and that I was a super strong candidate. That cheered me up, but didn't make my decision any easier as I drove home thinking of what to tell my wife about the whole experience. And the prospects. As it turned out, the choice wasn't up to me. Whew!

I have a recurring nightmare about a work environment I couldn't tolerate. It's based on a movie I saw once. I used to watch a lot of movies, and used to know what movie this was from, but it starts with an accountant at his desk, pulling the lever on his adding machine to crunch the numbers. It's a rather old movie, yes. The camera pans out and as it does, there are several accountants all pulling their levers at the same time. As the camera pans out even further, you see a warehouse sized room full of accountants, all sitting at desks in neat rows and columns, all pulling on their adding machine levers at the same time. Hours on end, day after day. Twenty years. All for a gold watch. That may not be everyone's idea of a nightmare, but it scares the you know what out of me.

Sometimes there is legitimately a bad fit between you and the job. Maybe you've applied with an international conglomerate that does business all over the world and while you have a perfect pedigree otherwise, they are really in need of someone who is bilingual in English and Mandarin so they can expand their Chinese business market several years down the road. "But I speak French!" you say. Fortunately, you realize that speaking French is absolutely nothing like speaking Chinese and that you just don't want to work in a job where you can't communicate. You are also smart enough to know that when they have the choice between you and someone who already is fluent and conversant in the appropriate lingo, you are on the losing side of the balance beam. That was easy, but you still might want to take a vacation in China one day. And begin looking for companies with branches in France.

In college I had a minor in Museum Studies and applied for positions with a number of history and natural history museums. Not to any open positions mind you, just on a fishing expedition, letting them know that when they had an opening, I was their man. I figured this was a long shot, especially since I was sending these letters to places like the Smithsonian.

One day I got an astounding call. The head of the public relations office at one of these great places called and wanted me to come talk about a job. It was awesome, a maritime museum in New England. As a kid I'd been to this place many times and the family had a connection in that my father had grown up in the shadow of one of the ships on display here.

We talked and toured and I was in hog heaven. But I realized that this was a job I could not take, no matter how much I wanted to work there. You see, the job involved driving all over New England marketing to school districts to get them to send groups of students on educational class trips to this site. I wanted to be at the museum, not driving all over the countryside, and I turned it down. That kind of opportunity never came my way again.

Fresh out of graduate school I came across a very intriguing job posting in *The New York Times*. The organization was looking for college graduates with a desire to be patriots. Foreign language training would be beneficial as assignment overseas was very likely. There wasn't a great deal of description as to the actual job duties, but it sounded rather adventurous. And yes, it was with the Central Intelligence Agency.

Dang! I can be James Bond I thought. Fast cars. Beautiful women. Martinis shaken, not stirred. That line of thinking may have been a tad bit romanticized on my part. It seems that CIA employees aren't all deep cover spies. And even the real spies don't all live like 007.

I sent off a letter of introduction and a resume. Several weeks later, after I had sort of forgotten about being a superhero, I got a call from a nice lady who wanted me to make another phone call to speak with someone about my resume. She gave me his number, and his name. Being of eastern European descent myself, I am certainly in no position to make fun of anyone's name, but this guy's was a real doozy. The nice lady had to say it several times, and spell it several more. I thought to myself, "how the hell am I gonna call this guy when I can't even say his name?"

Just do your best. They will correct you if you are wrong. If it is a difficult name, they are probably used to it and won't hold it against you.

After rehearsing the name and getting it down pretty well, I dialed the number ready to speak of spies. Of course when the man answered the phone I butchered his name horribly, but he didn't even seem to notice. Maybe it wasn't really his name. We talked about the job.

OOOh, sounds interesting. Then we began to talk about the process. I should have known- Feds. There was this interview, then an application, then a small background check, then another interview, then another, more detailed background check. Then another interview, then some training on how to deal with torture and all the secret spy stuff. I still can't give you details of what the job was- I'd have to kill you then.

Listening to this list of hurdles and hoops I'm thinking to myself, "gee, this could take a while and I need a job now!" I also remembered that when my brother joined the Air Force, doing some weird kind of job, the FBI came snooping around the neighborhood asking lots of questions and all the neighbors thought he was on the ten most wanted list. This might be a good opportunity, but it isn't worth all this to me. I told the man so, and that was that. He seemed a little irritated with me and for a long time I was always looking over my shoulder.

Any good fisherman can tell you that the story of "the one that got away" is one in which you are encouraged to embellish the facts with some personal spin. With this in mind, all of these jobs, which for whatever twisted and poorly grounded logic rejected you, become a tale of wise decision making on your part. That job, that company, none of it was good enough for you.

- **You don't have to accept the job.**

- Interviews are a process for you to see if you like the company as much as for the company to evaluate you.
- Sometimes "stuff" gets in the way.

Chapter 8
Hell No, I Won't Go!

There are many jobs that I know I would not want to do, and so naturally I wouldn't waste my time, or anyone else's applying for them. We all have certain limits which would require extremely desperate times to broaden. I don't want to work in the fish canning industry, slicing up dead fish and being elbow deep in their innards and knee deep in blood. Nor do I want to be a ski lift operator. I'd get to see lots of cute snow bunnies, but I would freeze my burr off in the cold. Besides, I'd rather be skiing!

Then again, sometimes you will find that with a little more thought or exploration of the job in its actuality, you will come to realize that things aren't always what you might think. Something you thought you would like might not be exactly as envisioned, and occupations you thought you would never like could turn out to be interesting.

You may have gathered that I derive some pleasure from writing. Very true, and I once interviewed for a position as a magazine feature writer. I'd seen the ad in the newspaper for a writer with a financial magazine and figured the MBA and my passion for writing, as well as previous publishing experience, would qualify me for at least an interview.

The editor called me a few days later and said he loved the writing samples I'd submitted and wanted me to come to his office to talk with him. After a long conversation he offered me the job, and then a piece of advice he wanted me to consider before giving him an answer.

What he told me was that sometimes when our passion becomes our job, it can lose some of its glamour. My love for writing up until then hadn't been accompanied by the daily pressure of meeting deadlines, extensively editing copy, always having another story in my back pocket, or being forced to write on assignment about a topic which held little interest for me. I've since learned that I'd rather write about what I want to write about, and on my own timetable.

Coming from the other direction, I had a job once as an administrator overseeing a number of departments, including some support areas. I was movin' on up, toward the top of the heap! Or so I thought. Turned out that I was much happier getting my hands dirty with some of the physical labor than sitting with good posture in my ergonomically incorrect leather executive chair, pushing a pencil across some high level memo directing everyone to be ever vigilant about the overuse of paperclips in hard economic times.

The bottom line is, if you see something that interests you, try for it. You may find a new calling. You may even find that others see your abilities in this new endeavor. Could be that you still think you want to pursue this field, even if the employers don't agree with you on your capabilities. Or, maybe after checking it out, you decide it might be a good hobby. Or it might be best left alone. You won't know if you never take a chance.

- **If it looks interesting, apply.**
- **Closer inspection may show you something you didn't see before.**
- **You can always change your mind.**

Chapter 9
The Sure Thing

There is no such thing as a sure thing. There is always some degree of uncertainty and risk. I know that when I was hiring people, I wrote several job descriptions so that only one person in the world could do the job- the one person I wanted to hire. You are required to do that sometimes when you are forced, legally, to advertise the job, but know exactly who you want already. Happens all the time, especially in education and government. You have to be really careful so no one else slips through the cracks who might actually have good credentials.

As a jobseeker, you have to keep this in mind because no matter how well qualified you think you are, there is no guarantee that you will get hired. Here is an example of how that could occur when the search committee isn't quite sure of what they want to do.

I had seen a job advertised for a business manager at a local nonprofit. I saw it, read it and debated it in my mind. Is that really something I wanted to do? After about three weeks, and still seeing this opening freshly advertised, I decided that I should apply- I could always turn it down. Assuming I even got an interview.

They called the same day I sent in my packet and scheduled a meeting. When I arrived, they wanted me to fill out an application. I'd arrived early just for that purpose, but who knew it would take an hour to fill out the 27 pages of forms? That put me almost thirty minutes late for the interview. But since they knew I was there early and working on the forms I figured that wouldn't be so bad. They greeted me warmly when I went into the conference room where we were to meet, but I could sense something funny. Not humorous mind you, odd. I know I had checked my collar buttons, and my tie, and my fly. Was I overdressed? They were wearing casual attire and I was in my suit. No, I thought, this job requires a suit for the interview. I finally put my finger on it- they were bored! They were just going through the motions, or so I suspected.

I did all the things you do- smile, shake hands, say thank you, express interest and send a follow-up note. On this one I even had two people I knew put in a call to the boss to give me an extra boost. That's how I found out. One of these folks was friends with the HR director. My interview was Friday afternoon, Memorial Day weekend, and what I found out was that someone had started working in the position by Wednesday, the first week of June. They had made that decision before I interviewed.

This was just a case of "we're pretty sure we've got who we want, but let's check out this new applicant just to be sure." As it turned out, they could have saved me, and themselves, a lot of time and effort. Don't want to work for an organization that can't make decisions.

Regardless of how well everything goes, how well you seem to fit the job, how well you fit the corporate culture, how well you fit in with the coworkers, you need to keep your guard up to some degree. There was a time I was interviewing for a position with the state government which would have given me the opportunity to be a small business consultant. It was a long process and I was actually on my second interview. I had met with the search committee in the local office, and was now meeting with another group at the higher, state office level. Success here equated to a ticket to ride. Mind you now, I said I would have become a SMALL business consultant.

At the very end of the interview, something was said and I replied, kind of off the cuff, something to the effect that we weren't dealing with IBM here. The head of the committee looked at me and said, "but they could be some day." I sheepishly agreed and realized right away that she was highly offended by the comment she had perceived to be a slight toward small businesses. That was certainly not my intention, but it cost me big time. Not only did I not get the job that time, but in the future, as I applied for several other positions in this agency, this woman's negative impression of me seemed to be written in stone in the organizational hiring manual. Although several years later I did get another interview with this group, the damage was done and I had no chance. Some poor lower echelon, field level manager who hadn't read that page of the manual had let me slip in the cracks because, well, because my qualifications justified an interview. C'est la vie!

Another scenario is when you are just positive that you are "the one". You have a gut feeling telling you this, but there is also some outside corroboration of that.

I worked with a placement agency for a while but didn't have much success that way. I did have two interviews for good jobs, but in each case odd things happened. Both times the agency had set something up for me to meet with a representative of their client company, and my conversations with the agency director were my outside corroboration. He told me the client was thrilled and was eager to have me; the interview was just a formality.

The first time I went, met, talked, toured, answered all the questions. I had a lock on this job, and it was a pretty good one.

The company was a high tech manufacturer working on the latest innovation in the recording business. It was about a thirty minute drive, but I was impressed by the operation. I had to wear a space suit to go into a clean room during the facility tour.

I left the interview and went back to talk to the agency manager who had since spoken with the company HR guy about bringing me on. I was stunned- they didn't want to hire me because I seemed too cocky, too self assured that I already had the job. Not hungry enough. And sure enough, they didn't hire me. They later went out of business, and lots of people lost their jobs, including one of my neighbors.

The second opportunity the agent set me up with was even better. This was a little closer to home and the hours and pay would be better. Again, the hunch and the outside source of optimism for success. And this time, there was a second source of optimism. The company itself told me they wanted to hire me. We talked money and start dates and all the little details. Then one day, before I started, they called to say that the economy sucked and business was down. There was a hiring freeze going into effect the day before I was to start. Even though the guy who would be my boss tried to say I was already a done deal, his bosses disagreed and stopped the process dead in its tracks. The hiring freeze never came off and the business eventually traded hands. They are still in operation, I think, but on a much smaller scale and with a new focus of emphasis.

The moral of the story is to not count your chickens before the eggs crack. You may have a great interview which hurtles you to the head of the competition. The company may love you. You might even get an offer of a job. But, until you actually walk through the door as the company's newest employee and get to work, you ain't got the job. And even then, you have to do the job to keep the job.

As a rising college senior, I needed a summer job while I took a couple of classes. I found one delivering flowers for a florist in a major metropolitan area. They gave me the flowers, gave me a car, told me where to go and sent me on my merry way. I was reasonably familiar with the city streets, and they were laid out in a very orderly manner so no place would be too hard to find. Only problem was, they gave me a little VW Beetle with a stick shift. The Beetle was cool, but I'd spent about eight minutes of my life driving a stick. I was a mess. I stalled. I bucked. I drove with the parking brake on and stalled more. It took all day to do the morning deliveries and when I got back to the shop, the owner and I agreed that it wasn't going to work. That egg hatched into a chicken, but it ran away and left me unemployed again.

- **Don't assume anything.**
- **Always give it your best shot.**
- **Don't count on anything, until it is firmly in your grip.**

Chapter 10
How's This Group Gonna Work?

My wife ways she admires me greatly for being able to handle so many different types of interviews. She is an accountant and has basically had one job for the last twenty years. When she got that job, she met with one person who asked her some accounting questions and a few nicety questions about her background, then offered her the job. I wish it was all so simple, but I have never had an interview like that.

The most common thing I've seen is a group interview. There are several variations, but basically, there is a leader of the group who contacts you to set up the appointment and greets you on arrival. It may actually be that person's representative who does this, but the leader has the responsibility. You then meet with "the group," which is generally made up of the various stakeholders in the position. This means you will meet with subordinates, peers and superiors, all of whom have some degree of say in the selection.

You may not realize who fits each role until the introductions are made so never judge a book by its cover. Just because a person is dressed very casually in a group doesn't mean s/he isn't the president of the company.

Generally the group leader will talk for a moment about how things will go, that is, who will ask what when, or what order people will speak. It may be that they all want to tell you all about themselves and their role in the organization, then about the job, and then ask questions of you. Or it may be that they just want to ask questions of you. Or, it may just kind of be a freewheeling general discussion. The type of interview often gives you a little bit of a glimpse into the nature of the organization.

The more formal the interview, the more formal the company. If you notice that everyone looks to the leader before asking a question or making a comment, then the leader holds all the power. If the conversation is very free flowing, then it may be that the organization is very open to participation at all levels, or that there is no real structure. In either case, or any median scenario, you need to get a feel for this and be able to make your own determination as to how comfortable you are with such a structure. Both scenarios have their pluses and minuses, and either may get on your nerves.

Another type of group interview is a kind of traveling adventure. Initially you will meet with one or two people who conduct the bulk of the interview, and then move on to other constituencies. Most likely, the sequence of people you meet will be somewhat random, based on their availability at any particular moment.

I once had an interview in the mountains of Virginia where the schedule called for me to meet with the human resources representative first, then the individual who would be my boss, then his boss, then the people who would be working for me, and then anyone else who happened to be interested in talking to me, either from inside or outside of the company. Because the boss's boss was busy, his slot on the schedule was moved and I got to talk to some subordinates first.

In this situation it was just a matter of giving everyone the opportunity to meet with me and get a feel for what I was like. It was much more for their benefit than mine although meeting my boss's boss gave me the indication that he was all about him, and meeting with my would be subordinates gave me the impression that they would do whatever I asked of them, as long as they wanted to, or saw a benefit to themselves. There was no one present for the last part of the process, so the HR person and I decided that I could leave. I decided not to take that job based more on the feel I got for the community as a whole and how my family would feel there.

A variation of this progressive style of interview is a matter of checking the boxes and clearing the hurdles. A small southern university interviewed me once for a job that was very much in transition. I met with a lot of people, but later found out that each person was just checking the box to say they had met with me, rather than indicating that they had tried to formulate any kind of opinion. While I talked to everyone from the student intern in the ID card office all the way to the President of the College, I was never really in contention for the job.

I had driven six hours to get to the interview, and almost had to spend the night in some little town along the way because my car broke down. This is a really cool kind of aside story I just have to tell because of the warm and fuzzy it gives me whenever I think about it.

A few miles south of nowhere, I had just passed through the middle of a little town when the car's alternator finally gave up the ghost. My dashboard lights had been blinking at me for a while and I wasn't sure what was happening. One mechanic in the last little town I went through told me to just keep going. I think he was hoping it would quit outside his town so he could tell me it then needed a new engine.

For those of you not mechanically inclined, when the alternator quits, the engine gets no power and the car shuts down and will not start again until it gets a new alternator. I walked down the road looking for signs of life and flagged down a car coming out of a driveway. The man took me to his house and called a mechanic for me. He told me that he was a preacher and that the shop he called was the honest one in town. The wrecker came out after an hour or so and was going to load me onto the flatbed when I decided to try the car once more and it started. He followed me back to town and sure enough, along the way the damn thing quit again and I ended up on the wrecker anyway. Could have saved 50 bucks.

The folks at the fix it shop were real nice but told me they had to drive 40 miles to get the part and it looked like I was gonna be stayin' a while. They recommended a restaurant in town where I could get some lunch. I told them

I had to be 200 miles down the road by 8 AM the next day and they made a phone call to Cousin Bill who might be coming into town later. He agreed to the detour to get the part. He showed up several hours later and even though the shop was filled with cars far ahead of me in the queue, the mechanics put me to the head of the line and fixed me up. Just wonderful people in the most unexpected place.

So, back to the interview. They knew I was coming 300 miles for this interview, and they paid for the hotel and some food, but they never had any intention of giving me the job. Even as I left I thought I had done really well and was a strong contender.

I had sent a follow up letter to everyone I had talked to, as I always do, but was really anxious about this so I called a couple of days later to see how things were going. The man wouldn't take my call, his secretary saying he was busy. I called several days later and the man took the call, and had nothing but bad things to say.

He said I'd never really been in the running. He said they just brought me down because they needed to make it evident that they had spoken to several people, and selected the best, who they had pre-ordained. That can be confusing and devastating. But it's all part of the game. While there are some rules you must follow as an interviewee, there are fewer that the interviewers need follow, and being nice isn't one of them.

As another variation on the progressive interview, you may find yourself working your way up the chain of command, with each person along the way closely scrutinizing your every move and word, thereby forming an opinion to relay to the next level of the command structure.

A great job in an iffy location out of town offered me an opportunity to interview. It was such a good opportunity that I was definitely interested enough to drive five hours to an interview with no reimbursement for mileage or a hotel room.

Frequently glancing at the typewritten itinerary he had folded up in his shirt pocket, the interview emcee had a full day planned for me. We started at eight a.m. He was really the public relations person and had nothing to do with the position I was interviewing for. But he was a good talker. We conversed for a long time about the overall organization and where my position fit in and pretty much the nature of the job.

We took a long tour of the company campus, with him showing me all the buildings and telling me what went on there. He also introduced me to anyone he thought was relevant as we moved around the complex. We then took a tour of the community which gave me an opportunity to see some of the housing options, and to get the scoop on what the very small town was like. There was definitely some urban renewal going on, and much more needed, but it was a clean place. After the tour we ate lunch in the company cafeteria which gave me the opportunity to meet some of the mid level people in the company- very informal.

After lunch I began meetings with the higher ups. First was the PR guy's boss who actually had several areas under him. That was a weird meeting because it seemed to me that he really wasn't too interested in talking to me a whole lot. Maybe he was busy, but he only asked one or two questions about my background. I don't know if this is significant, but I remember his office as being very dark. He had a window, but the blinds were closed tight so no light came in, and he had only a desk lamp turned on although there was an overhead light available. Maybe he had a headache, or a hangover.

From there I moved on to the VP who I would fall under. He was an ex Marine and it was real obvious. Not only did he have all his commemorative plaques on his office wall, he still spoke in the very crisp and direct way of a senior Marine officer. If you've been in the service, you know what I mean. And everyone called him Colonel. I always wondered if Colonel Sanders had really been in the military.

He asked a lot of questions and was looking for short answers. His big question however was, "how much money do you want to do this job?" As he put it, if my answer was wrong, it was nice to have met me, but beyond the handshake, there was no further point for discussion. I'll talk about how to answer this question later in more detail, but for now lets say we went back and forth with generalities until he pinned me down with needing a very specific answer.

Earlier in the day I had been told that I would be meeting with all of these people and then the Senior Vice President, and then, if he had time, the President. I hadn't realized it until several days, or weeks later, but each of my stops was a check off point. If I failed the test at one spot, the game was over and I would not pass go. After a somewhat lengthy delay, I was introduced to the Senior Vice President. His office was also dark. Should that have told me something about the corporate culture?

He asked me a number of questions and told me a great deal about the company and its higher philosophies. Up until this point people had talked about nuts and bolts things, but now we were moving into the stratosphere, most of which I knew would be way beyond my pay grade. I listened intently and finally he asked me if I had any questions. I told him what a wonderful day I had had, and how everyone was so nice and informative and no, I didn't have any unanswered questions at that time.

It was from this experience that I learned that I should always, always have another question in my back pocket, even if was not real important, or had been previously answered. Having questions shows inquisitiveness, the ability to think, and most of all, a great interest in what's going on.

The Senior Veep thanked me for coming and said he would check with the President on his schedule. By this time it was already 4 PM. As instructed, I waited, sitting in a hard wooden chair in the hallway. There were a number of doors in the hall, all without any indication as to who or what lay beyond them. People walked by, in and out of the doors, and never failed to stare at me. I smiled. Was the President's office behind one of those doors?

At the end of 30 minutes, a woman came out and said the President would not be able to meet with me. She thanked me for coming and said I'd be hearing from them. That was it. Kinda awkward, huh? And just plain bizarre when I never did hear from them, one way or the other.

As it turned out, the President didn't have time to see me that day because as I moved through the chain of command, a decision was made at some point that I was not going to be the first choice, and so, the President wasn't going to waste his time.

- **Study the dynamics of the group for clues about the job and company.**
- **Understand who is who, and what your progress through the process means.**
- **Always have a spare question ready.**

Chapter 11
One On One And Other Group Alternatives

It seems that the one on one, one shot deal is fading from popularity. It used to be that this was the workhorse type of interview where you met with the person you would work for, they would give the thumbs up or down, and that would be that. But these days no one wants to make a decision by themselves. No one wants to be responsible if somehow a dud gets hired, so they spread the blame, and glory, around by doing the group things.

In a one on one, you have to really be sure you hit it off with the person on the other side of the desk. You'll be working with them, and perhaps only them. If it gets off to a bad start, you may never recover. You should be able to pick up on this one sometime after the interview starts, but of course by then it's too late and you sit there asking yourself why you are wasting your time. I'll give you an example.

I had seen an ad for a building products sales person that sounded interesting. I sent in a resume, and since I had four years experience as a building service professional, I figured I had a pretty good shot at it. At least I got the interview, but this one turned out to not be worth the time it took to drive up there. When I arrived, I was warmly greeted and offered a seat in the office of my prospective boss. He proceeded to tell me that his interviewing style was to just talk, and that I should feel free to jump in any time. This was early in my interview career and I was more used to structured meetings, but what the hell, right?

As it turned out, this guy talked about himself for an hour, and then asked if I had anything to add. The whole time I'm thinking to myself, "you should say something man." But he was talking so fast that by the time I could form a word on my lips, he had switched subjects completely. When he asked me if I had anything to add, I wasn't sure whether he was looking for me to add some sort of praise about him for his future use, or to say something about myself, so I looked at him for a second and said, "I really didn't get a chance to say anything, but blah, blah, blah, this is why I'd be good for the job." I don't think he heard any of that- he was looking in the mirror as I walked out the door.

Of course, if you click well right away, it goes much better. It's easier to talk comfortably and freely when you are cozy with the other party. In my current position, my boss and I hit it off right away. We have several things in common in our backgrounds and personalities, and it is really great working with this guy.

A tool that employers use to save money and time in screening applicants is the telephone interview. This can be very uncomfortable for some people, primarily because you can't see the other person. I can just imagine them rolling their eyes at my answers or making unpleasant hand gestures.

One of my issues with a telephone interview is waiting for the phone to ring if they are calling me. I worry that someone else will call, and my line will be busy when the important call comes through. In this particular case I wasn't necessarily expecting a call, but one came while I was in the garage at home doing some weight lifting. There was no phone in the garage itself, so when I heard the one inside ringing I had to run in to get it. I felt a little dorky telling the interviewer on the other end that I was all out of breath because I had just come from the gym. What kind of person gives the phone number for a gym as an employment contact? Is that like giving Joe's Bar as a contact? Or, if I have a gym at home, how much do I need a job? Or even, what kind of situation is this person in if he has time to hang out in his home gym during the day in the middle of the work week? All questions some might ask, but which can easily throw false impressions into the mix.

I worry about how to sit, and where, if I'm interviewing on the phone. Do you want to be really comfortable, like with your feet hung over the arm of a big overstuffed chair, or do you want to sit in a semi uncomfortable straight back chair? Does it matter? Certainly the other person doesn't care, but will one level of comfort or another effect your answer? Or how you sound? Same thoughts apply to how you dress. Would it be ok to interview in your underwear, without shaving? Or nude? Or should you try to look professional? Who are you impressing? I think the bottom line on these issues is that no one answer is right or wrong- this one really depends on what helps you perform your best. Of course, if the "phone call" is really an online chat, with video, the answers to all of these questions become a little more obvious. In this case, you need to look your best as well as put on your best performance.

Along the same lines is the teleconferenced interview where you meet with a live person or two, and some talking heads. The funny thing about this is that the images are almost always blurry so it's hard to tell what people look like let alone what their expressions are. If that is what you see, you know they see you the same way so that time spent getting every hair perfectly placed was probably wasted. The other strange part about this is that depending on the sound system, you may very well get the impression that you are in an old Asian movie that has been translated and overdubbed for the US market. Mouths will move, but sounds follow sometime later rather than occur simultaneously. So the question is asked and then you get a blank stare while you are forced to delay your answer until you hear the question. Until everyone realizes what's going on it can be pretty funny. Gut wrenching funny.

Meeting over lunch is a possibility that is sometimes used when the interviewers are very busy and have to cram business into every waking moment of the day. While it might seem on the surface that an interview over a meal might be easy, it poses its own set of challenges and difficulties. Sometimes when you are young, poor, unemployed, greedy, gluttonous or just plain naïve, this seems like a great deal. In reality, it might be a nightmare.

Fresh out of graduate school I managed to get myself an interview with a cruise line for a position as a sales rep to travel agencies. Awesome. I love boats and ships, and exotic places, and how hard could it be? Oh, woe was me as I was quite unprepared.

When you get a job, people don't usually expect you to be 100 percent up to speed on the first day. There are a lot of things you need to learn. Maybe about the job and the tasks involved, or just maybe things about the corporate culture or quirks about how they do things. But some things you are expected to know in advance, or be capable of.

I was nervous about this interview, as I always used to be about interviews. Of course I wanted to make a good impression so there was the suit and tie and portfolio. Questions at the ready. But damn if the spaghetti I ordered for my meal didn't get all over my shirt. Lesson learned- mealtime interviews aren't necessarily for eating; and don't order messy food. I really didn't have that outgoing sales personality at the time, or hadn't learned to come across that way, so I wasn't cut out for the job, but if the spaghetti sauce hadn't made such a mess of me I might have had a better chance.

Your mother told you not to talk with your mouth full, so if you eat during an interview, even if it is something neat like a dainty little salad, it's hard to ask or answer lots of questions while dining. If you have all day, that's one thing, but if you're doing a mealtime interview because everyone is so busy, forget it.

One used to hear a lot about the three martini lunch in the corporate world, but I'm not sure how widespread that is in these days and times. I'm sure there are still some people who manage to combine alcohol with a lunch occasionally, but many companies have rules prohibiting drug and alcohol use during working hours and many will even conduct random testing. It may not be so random if you show up stinking of gin and babbling incoherently. I know we had some champagne at a reception once when we dedicated a new building, but that's another story. The real point is, NEVER order a drink during an interview lunch. Even if everyone else does. You are trying to put your best foot forward so don't expose yourself to an opportunity to put that foot squarely in your mouth. Of course you want to seem like you fit into the corporate culture at this possible employer and wisely so, but you can be "one of the gang" later, after you get the job. Until then, you need to look and act professional.

Now here's a real grabber that almost makes me wonder whether interviewers and restaurants are in cahoots, or if other forces beyond our control come into play, bringing with them a sick sense of humor. I was in the job market, as usual, and I met a guy I knew for lunch at a steak and burger kind of place. We were going to talk job hunting strategy and sales techniques. He had a sense of humor I didn't always understand, but he was a good guy and offered to buy me lunch to talk. He ordered the fish and I just got a burger. One thing I had learned was that even on someone else's dime you don't order the most expensive dish.

When the food came out, my plate had a giant bun and some lovely lettuce and tomato and all the fixings, but there was no burger. The waiter had come in and out so swiftly I had no chance to say anything. My companion and I looked at each other and wondered aloud if the burgers were so fine that when cooked to order, they were presented separately with great pomp and circumstance. We waited, and nothing further happened. Finally, we got the waiter and told him what had happened and of course he was devastated and got me a burger rather quickly. But this sort of thing is, to say the least, a little out of the ordinary, and if you aren't fully prepared for anything and everything, this could really throw you off your game.

- **There are many formats to prepare for.**
- **Find out in advance, as best you can, the who, what, when, where and how of the meeting.**
- **Be prepared.**

Chapter 12
Meet the Competition

You cannot control who the other job applicants are. When a job is posted, whether through the grapevine, on the internet, through some in house type organ or in the newspaper, anyone who finds the listing can apply. And frequently do.

There will always be competition. Remember that each person is an individual with their own strengths and weaknesses. Some strengths may be totally unrelated to the job, but still carry tremendous weight. Regardless of their qualifications, certain people are sometimes invited to put their hat in the ring.

From my way of thinking, if you are invited to apply, your odds for successfully capturing the position have gone up dramatically. But remember, there is no such thing as a sure thing. If an old classmate of yours knows you've been working in some field relevant to what he's hiring for, an invite might be extended. However, the details and nuances of your area of expertise may not quite mesh with what is needed, and one or the other of you will realize that and back away. Maybe that colleague is interested in bringing you on board, but doesn't have a position that meets your salary needs.

On the other hand, as I once discovered in competing against someone's old coworker, the bonds of friendship and collegiality can be stronger than good qualifications.

I applied for a new position within the company I was currently working for. This would have been a promotion, and in an area I had a great deal of experience with. When I was called back for a second interview, I thought I had a pretty good lock on the job. After all, employers only want to talk twice to people they have a strong feeling about. The second interview involved meeting with some different people from the first interview. This time it was subordinates, and the behavior of the person I would be working most closely with gave it all away.

The "boss" had asked this person to show me what she did, and to grill me on my qualifications for the job. She showed me a few papers she pushed around and then said she was going to lunch. I questioned her as to whether she had questions she wanted to ask of me and she smiled. Then she told me that the second person they were considering for the job had no experience in this industry, but did know a little about the field. "HA!" I thought, "It's mine." Then she told me that this person and the boss had worked together in another industry for over twenty years and they were each looking forward to working together again. "ARGH!" I thought. And I was right, I didn't get the job.

Deep down you know, even if you don't want to admit it, that you can't always be the best at everything. Somewhere out there people exist who may actually be better candidates than you for some job. You have to do your best; the possibility of losing out to a truly better qualified person does exist. Coming in second, or worse, is always unpleasant, but the sting is a little easier to bear knowing that you really weren't the best.

Best or not, I experienced this very strange thing on several occasions. When a search committee has multiple candidates to meet with, they may opt to block out big chunks of time during the day to handle several meetings, allotting each candidate a portion of the total time period. In this case, you may unexpectedly get to meet the competition.

I was sitting in the reception area waiting for my appointed meeting time. The secretary told me the committee was running a little late. What she didn't tell me was that they were late because they were still with the person scheduled before me. What she further failed to tell me was that they were all in the room next door, and that the only way to get out of that room was to come through the room I was in, passing within inches of my feet as I sat in a chair. Apparently the search committee didn't realize they were behind because when they burst through the door, the leader looked at me and said, "OOOPS, Awkward situation!" Indeed it was, but it gives you a chance to look at the other person and identify all the ways in which you are superior to them. You can't always tell just by looking, but in my case, I was correct!

- **Don't worry about the competition, this is your interview.**

- Be polite if you happen to meet the other contenders.
- Know that the best person doesn't always get the job.

Chapter 13
What Would You Like to Know?

You know that your interviewers will want to ask a lot of questions of you to find out more about your background or suitability. When you hear them, you could feel every muscle in your body becoming taught. Sweat may bead up on your forehead or the palms of your balled up fists. Do you suddenly feel very thirsty and an irresistible urge to tug at your collar? Relax!

Sure, it's your big interview. And your proper behavior is crucial to your success. But because that behavior is so important, you gotta relax. If they see you squirming, you're finished. Cat got your tongue? Looks bad for you. The interview and its accompanying questions are not an inquisition, and the people on the other side of the desk are not out to get you. Think of this as your first opportunity to be a member of the team. Show them what you've got!

There are three main types of questions to be prepared for at an interview- the ones they ask, the ones you ask, and the ones that get overlooked. The last category can be the most dangerous because it always seems to happen that you will look back at some point and ask yourself why you didn't find out the answer to that question. Unfortunately, what these overlooked questions might be doesn't become apparent until it's too late.

In one position I held with a small private firm whose finances were somewhere near the outer limits of solvency, I was hired as the director to fix the fiscal problems through any means necessary. The only stumbling block was that they were more interested in having me redesign forms than in seeking out new market segments. They wanted me to generate instant cash flow at the expense of ever really fixing anything. I was constantly reminded by the team leader reporting to me that she had told me to find out, before I took the job, why there was such high turnover in my position. She was right, and I believe it was because people kept getting fired from the spot after getting fed up. Didn't work, and I was short lived there.

You can tell a lot about an organization, and the people who work there, by the types of questions they ask you during an interview. There are a number of standard questions you should expect to hear, and we'll look at them in a minute, but if you are lucky you may be introduced to something a little different that might actually make you think on your feet.

After many interviews for which I spent hours practicing, I stopped practicing so much. I'd pace the halls at home muttering the answers to questions I thought I might be asked. I'd ride in my car, radio off, spewing forth what I thought were good, if somewhat contrived, answers. And usually I sounded like I was reciting a memorized speech. By that time I knew the patter cold and figured that since we'd be largely discussing my life and experiences, I should have a pretty good command of the subject by now.

Don't get me wrong, I still reviewed my answers to the basic questions, and tried to remember some of the best off the wall one's I'd ever heard.

Some interviews are very stiff, and for me, indicative of a culture where I probably wouldn't be real happy. Cut and dry. Boring. Sometimes not getting the job is the best thing. You get questions like, "what college degree do you have?" or "how many years experience do you have in this field?" Or the dreaded one- "where would you like to be five or ten years from now." These are all valid questions. But, the best interviews allow for generating new questions and extemporaneous speaking. A candid flow of ideas and information.

- **Be prepared for questions of type 1 and 2 at all times. Avoid type 3 at all costs!**
- **Relax.**
- **Make it enjoyable.**

Chapter 14
You Tell Us

There are certain questions that are so basic in interviews that it is almost inconceivable that they will not be asked of you at every meeting. You should expect to be asked these, and you should have an answer ready. Your well rehearsed response will show that you are prepared, and know how to think.

Tell Us About Yourself

The very first interview question I ever had was, "tell me about yourself," and that, dear reader, is a question you can count on hearing at every interview. It's one of the most basic, yet most important simply because it gives the employer a chance to hear a summation of your qualifications, and to hear you put together some thoughts in a coherent manner. It's also your opportunity to shine. You need to make this an occasion to show them who you are, what you can do, and how you can help them.

The first time I heard this question, I made a horrible blunder and asked what they wanted to know. Tell them what **you** want **them** to know, and that is how great you are! Over the years, having lots of practice with this one and many chances to edit my answer, I finally came upon one which must work pretty well as I once sealed the deal just with my answer to this. Break your answer down into four sections.

Start by describing your education. You can make it as simple as "I have a bachelor's degree in Accounting" if you like. I don't necessarily tell where I went to school, it's on the resume. Besides, it's disquieting to see or hear a reaction like, "I never heard of that school." Unless you went to an A number one top tier school, you don't need to mention it. You can also leave out the details of every course you took, unless there is something that has real relevance to the job. If you apply for an accounting job, and have an accounting degree, they will correctly surmise that you took Intro I and II.

Do also mention advanced degrees and any certificates or special recognitions you have earned. Just keep in mind that hiring people don't always know what an Einstein Fellow at Cal Tech is when you apply for a job in advertising. What I like to say is something to the effect of, "this education gives me the technical skills to do the job, but also taught me how to think and to learn and communicate. Thus I can learn anything I need to for this job."

Segue from your education into your real world work experience. There is no need for tremendous detail here, but you do want to provide the basics like the name of the company, your title there, what you did and how long you were there. What you are trying to accomplish here is not to list all your previous jobs, or create a laundry list of the tasks you did, but to demonstrate how what you've done in the past can be beneficial to the employer in the future. Enumerate your skills.

My spiel at this point goes something like this, "when I got out of graduate school I went into the Navy as a Supply Corps officer where I helped to manage the business side of the Navy. I was on active duty for 5 years during which I was stationed aboard two ships and a naval air station. My responsibilities included managing retail operations, food services, housing, purchasing, contracting, inventory control, and services such as laundries and barbershops. My supervisory duties included managing up to 50 personnel. I also spent seven years in the reserves. After that….:"

In a similar way you go through the progression of each of your jobs. What I've explained to even someone who doesn't know much about the Navy is that I was an officer, or middle manager, who successfully managed a number of areas and a lot of people under difficult circumstances for a reasonably long period of time. So, I'm educated, stable, a leader, and experienced. Some people like to do this in chronological order, and some prefer a reverse listing. I like to do it from start to finish so that my listener will see how my experience builds.

No need to explain why you left a job unless you are asked. I left the Navy because my wife wanted to settle down in one place to start a family, but the Navy wanted me to go back to sea. Be prepared however, to give an explanation, especially for anything that might look a little suspicious. We'll talk about that soon.

Once you've given them all this history, you want to give a quick rendition of your strengths. They'll probably ask that tired old question again, "what are your strengths and weaknesses?" but hit them right away with strengths. You want to sound positive, and strong. You decide what your strengths are, but don't lie. And be sure they are relevant to the job you're applying for. Being good at crossword puzzles won't be very helpful in too many jobs, but it is a good strength to keep your mind sharp. Don't mention that. Stick to things like hard worker and detail oriented. Like I said, relevant to the job. Accountants don't need to be artistically creative.

Finally, tell them what you are looking for in a job or career. And then tell them how the position you are discussing fits in with those plans. Remember, they want to hire someone who will do a good job for them, and also who will be happy working there and will stay for a while. It costs a lot of money to hire and train someone to find out in a few weeks or months or sometimes even a few years that they are leaving for greener pastures. Say something about how you want to learn and grow in the future, what skills you'd like to develop, what career path you'd like to take. Again, you don't have to be real detailed, like giving them an exact chronology of what you want to do every day over the next ten years.

I know I said four parts, but there really is a fifth which kind of throws the ball back into their court for them. Remember, this is more than the 2 minute elevator resume, but you don't want to go on so long as to bore them.

When you are all finished, how do they know you are done? Say, "I know that was quick and abbreviated, so if you have any questions you'd like to ask, or would like more details, I'd be happy to answer." Or something like that. The answer I developed to this question could sometimes take as long as fifteen minutes to get through. That's really too long, but the time was sometimes effected by the actual pace of my speaking. I could do it in five minutes if I was really on a roll, and felt really good. If your answer is long like that, you could say that it reflects the highlights of your career rather than a quick and abbreviated summary. Just offer them a chance to ask further questions. They're going to ask all the questions they want regardless of your offer, but this way you feel like you have a little more control of the situation and can direct the conversation along a line beneficial to you.

You may have already answered all their questions and they won't ask any more. Or they may want additional details. Or they may feel a need to get their money's worth and proceed with their list of questions. Try to make it conversational if you are more comfortable that way. Maybe they aren't, and wont.

Multipurpose

Efficiency is a key element of success in business operations although everyone knows that the efficiency expert is not always the workingman's best friend. It does however provide a good basis for maximizing the utility of the available labor, machinery and time to create the maximum output. This same strategy can be used in developing answers to interview questions.

When I was in college, my junior year I think, I took a number of courses within my major. Each class required either a paper or a project and I spent quite a bit of time trying to figure out what kind of effort I could turn in that would be equally applicable to all of these classes. I ended up settling on a topic related to historical farming communities and was able to get three papers out of it, with minimal reworking for each separate paper. I've done the same thing with several interview questions.

The big question of tell us about yourself provides all the information you need to answer multiple forms of basically the same question. What are your qualifications? Why are you qualified? Why should we hire you? These questions are all pretty much the same. You need to talk about your education and experience. Strength of character and work ethics need to be mentioned. A description of what you want from your work and what you expect as a career path should be discussed. And then you need to tie it all together and tell them how and why all of that relates to the job they are looking to fill. Four questions, one answer. Pretty good.

If they ask you more than one of these questions, all you have to do is say something like, "We've discussed a great deal of the answer to this question previously, but blah, blah, blah." The blah, blah, blah of course gets replaced by your summation of education, experience, strengths, aptitude and desire for the position. Simple. You just have to be able to recognize the fact that your answer can be used for multiple questions, and to recognize one of the questions when you hear it in an alternate form.

- **Break your life into four segments, and make each segment valuable.**
- **Know how to use this information in many situations.**
- **Practice.**

Chapter 15
"We'd also like to know..."
Second Tier Questions

Once you get past the basic questions you know you will hear, there is a second set that you should anticipate because your answers offer the interviewers some excellent insight into your philosophy on work. You can reinforce your strengths here, and show how enthusiastic you are about the job and the company.

Why Come Here?

A difficult question can be, "why do you want to leave your current position?" or, "why did you leave?" There are all kinds of reasons: you got fired, the boss is a jerk, the pay stinks, the business closed. Maybe you just need a change of scenery. Who knows? Only you know the real reason, and you don't have to tell anyone that real reason if you don't want to. I can't tell you an exact answer but I can give you a couple of things to think about here.

The first thing is don't tell any outlandish lies, you will get caught. It may take a while, but you will get caught, and in a lot of companies that means you will get fired. It's usually easier to explain the truth, or to spin it a little, than to back out of a lie.

Suppose you were fired. That sounds bad and you might think it would automatically disqualify you. However, it may not be as bad as you think. In the broadest sense, the word "fired" conveys meaning along a spectrum of culpability. At one end of the spectrum, fired means you were booted on your butt for high crimes and treason. Fraud, theft and other truly criminal activities fall into this category. If you did something bad enough to go to prison, you might want to read another book after you finish this one.

On the other end of the spectrum, fired means you were let go due to no fault of your own. Sometimes people soften the tone by saying they were laid off. This happens when the company you work for hits a slow period and there isn't enough work for you to do. Or the economy is squeezing the company into downsizing some positions. If you are the third string player, whether because you aren't the sharpest tool in the shed or because your team is blessed with an abundance of talent, when it becomes evident that there is only money for two team players, you are the odd man out! No shame in that.

In between, there are a lot of people in the work world, and a multitude of reasons why any one of them might be fired. The two basic categories of reasons are that you did something not too good, or you did something much too good. Let me explain.

You might be axed for always being late, or looking like a bum. Are you just plain incompetent? There is no other book for you to read if that's the case, but there are other sources of help. Maybe you lipped off to the boss and in general have a bad attitude or poor people skills. These constitute doing something not too good.

Conversely, do you remember the kid in high school who always got a 100 on every test? That nerd messed up the grading curve every time! That kid is still out there in the workforce, and still not always popular. Maybe you are that kid and your boss, or a tenured coworker, still doesn't like you. Are you the one who always has the good ideas? That coworker feels threatened, and you are on the chopping block. This, I'm afraid, is an example of doing something much too good.

So when you say you were terminated there is a certain position you can take to elaborate, and it's not bent over at the waist. Provide an explanation. Give details if the job loss was innocent. Don't give so many details if the loss was your fault. The main thing is that you want to admit to what you did and then immediately go on to say that you have learned from that mistake and can honestly say it wouldn't happen again. Then try to switch back to your strengths. Many things can be forgiven or overlooked, but continuing dishonesty is not one of them.

Second thing is, don't say anything bad about your present employer. You don't want that to get back to them, and you don't want to look like you suffer from a case of sour grapes. I try to say that there are/were a lot of things I enjoyed in the position, including people or certain aspects of the work, but that you see this as an opportunity to move forward in your career. Even if the boss was a jerk, don't say that. He or she may not have offered enough mentoring or growth opportunities. You may have had philosophical differences. Maybe the organizational structure wasn't what you were looking for. There are many ways to describe a poor personal relationship in more positive terms.

There are lots of reasons to want to change jobs and you may have a very positive one. If not, spin your reasons into one. We all want more money. Indicate that you are looking for a promotion, or an opportunity to be better rewarded. If you use the reward theme, make sure you mention that it ain't just the money; you want to get more personal satisfaction out of the job. Along those lines you might have gotten bored in which case you say you are looking to enhance your skill set to make yourself more valuable in the workforce.

Strengths and Weaknesses

Even though you've already told the interviewers of your many strengths, they may very well ask again as a separate question. Strengths are usually combined with weaknesses in this question. Who the heck wants to admit to weaknesses anyway?

Start with strengths. Again, these need to be not just work related, but also specific to the job. And real. I vividly remember being asked once if I knew how to work with Excel. I had taken a continuing education class on that in the not too distant past so naturally I said, "Yes, I am familiar with Excel." On my first day of work, while my new boss was showing me some of the tasks I would be doing in my new position; one of the things he had to show me was how to get started with the program. Once I got it opened up I was good, I just didn't remember that small detail. And I felt like an idiot.

A laundry list of things you might mention, given the above criteria, includes creativity, detail orientation, strong communication skills, being a team player, an ability to see the big picture, punctuality, being a quick learner, having plenty of experience and working hard, just to name a few.

In discussing these strengths, it's imperative that you not just rattle them off without discussion. You need to go into some explanation of why and how this is a strength. Gauge the amount of time you have available for this discussion and give an example of how you used or demonstrated these strengths in the past. This is just another opportunity for you to toot your horn, to recap your qualifications and suitability. Use every opportunity to its fullest. And again, be sure the strengths you choose to stress are relevant to the job.

When you have to touch on weaknesses, you can't say you don't have any, or can't think of any. Everyone has some kind of weakness and no one will believe otherwise about you. So, let's figure out a weakness that isn't too weak, or might even be twisted around into a strength.

Mine is that I have a hard time allowing for others who are not as on the ball as me. I always qualify that by saying that I realize this is a weakness so I make an extra effort to keep an eye on this. To me, that shows that I am a number one player, but realize that not everyone is and I am considerate of them. Weakness, and strength. You might say something like, "I have a messy desk, but I know where everything is, and can maintain my detail orientation in spite of it." Weakness, strength. Of course, if the people interviewing you have immaculately organized desks and offices, you might not want to use that one, but consider another example instead.

Just don't say things like, "I'm always late," or "I'm a mean bastard," or "technology is totally beyond my grasp." You don't want to look like someone who no one wants to work with, will be a drag on the company, or is just a plain old mo-ron.

What Have You Done?

I've often been asked about my greatest accomplishments. This is a difficult question for me because there are so many! I used to be modest about all of this, but now I'm less hesitant to stress my good points. And there is nothing wrong with tooting your own horn, that's what they are looking for. You just want to be sure that you can talk about something that might in some way be relevant to the job. If your greatest accomplishment was to win the spelling bee in Mrs. Donaldson's fourth grade class your interviewer probably won't be too impressed. You have to think hard about this one. There must be something.

What I developed over time was an answer that listed several things, each of which demonstrated some particular aspect of my background. I would talk about earning a master's degree, being an officer in the navy, owning my own business, being a stable family man and then having accomplished a number of things in my career. Then, you have to talk about that something you did at work. Maybe you participated in a big project. Or perhaps you developed some new method of doing something. Did you suggest something that saved time or money? Maybe you just showed up every day and gave your all. If you think about it, there will be something, even if it doesn't seem very big. Just be sure that you have an answer thought out in advance. Being unprepared is an impression that is difficult to overcome.

On the very first day of second semester classes in grad school I got off to a very bad start in one of my classes which had a ripple effect through the school until I could overcome the bad impression I made. The instructor started right in with the lecture and discussion and asked me a question from the assigned reading. No excuse here, just a statement of fact, but I didn't know there was assigned reading since I didn't have a syllabus until I actually got to class. I made the mistake of not trying to BS my way through an answer and instead told the prof that I hadn't done the reading.

Good Gracious alive!!! That unleashed a real firestorm. How dare I come to class unprepared!!?? I was wasting the prof's time and my fellow student's time. I was a drag not only on the class but on all of society. I was doomed for failure. I felt a little guilty about not doing the reading in advance, but thought the guy got a little carried away with the apocalyptic nature of my faux pas. But other students were afraid to work in a group with me until they heard the other stories about me- hard work, dedication and good grades. Image is important.

- **Know who you are.**
- **Be prepared to tell people.**

Chapter 16
"A Little Thoughtfulness Now"
Third Tier Questions

With enough remaining time in your appointment, and a clever group of interviewers, you may run into a final group of questions. These are the kind of questions designed to see if you have thought about your life and how you have lived it. There aren't necessarily right or wrong answers. But a blank stare coming from you gives the poorly received impression that you do not understand your own inner workings very well.

How Do You Manage?

If you're going to be a manager, employers are looking for leadership and will often ask, "What is your management style?" I can't tell you what your style is, but I can say that what they are looking for is how do you treat people who work for you? Everyone has their own style, and some styles are better suited to certain jobs than others. A Marine gunny sergeant can't have management by consensus as his style; he has to be a strong and decisive leader who his troops will obey without question for their own safety under fire.

How do you develop teamwork and cooperation? What do you do when you have a disciplinary problem or performance issue with a particular employee? Do you love to hover over everyone's shoulder to constantly be checking on what they are doing? Can you let go and delegate assignments? Do you think there is a difference between delegating assignments and responsibilities? Do your employees like you? You may hear any or all of these as individual questions, and in some different forms, but you should understand how you gather information and make decisions, and how you make things work the way they should. And be prepared to explain your style.

Stressors

In today's work world, everyone encounters stress at some time. It may be purely work related, or may be combined with other parts of your life. What causes you to stress out, and how you deal with the stress, may be the topic of another question you will face.

The interviewers know that all of their employees have to deal with some sort of stress, but they expect that you won't let that stress impact your work performance. Thus, you need to assure them that such is the case when you are stressed. People have many ways of dealing with stress, from squeezing a stress ball to going for a five mile run. Maybe you need to scream, or crush something. In the workplace, the stress ball would be the preferred method from the employer's perspective. It's quiet, safe, and generally isn't disruptive. Those other options mentioned may work outside the workplace, but no one wants to see you bang your head on the cubicle wall.

They will also have reasonable expectations that you will not feel overwhelmed by minor irritations. A lousy selection in the candy machine can be annoying, but it shouldn't ruin your day. Rude and/or incompetent co-workers are also irksome, but shouldn't cause a total work stoppage. Major life crisis like serious health issues, divorce, and certain aspects of child rearing are a different story. Your boss still doesn't want your work to suffer because of these things, but you might get a little more sympathy and understanding under these circumstances. But not forever, and not repeatedly. You have to wonder how many grandmothers some people have after three or four of them die in a six month period.

Thus, in answering this question, as much as possible you need to indicate that little things don't rock your boat and you work hard to keep stress from bothering you. Stress is an obstacle that you face head on and work your way around. It's not an insurmountable roadblock.

What Tasks Float Your Boat?

When you hear the interviewer ask, "What do you like best/least about your current job, or some other job?" what they are looking for is a sense of what sort of tasks and work you like to do. Tell them what you like. If you like routine and repetitive work where you know day after day exactly what you'll be doing, say so. If you prefer to always have something new and different, tell them. Some people like deskwork and others prefer to be out and about. Perhaps you are a strongly people oriented person and love to interact with others. Someone else may prefer to work alone.

I prefer something in the middle where I have a list of things I'm trying to accomplish every day, but I never know what other tasks I might encounter during the day. That gives me some sense of order and stability, but not routine. I like to always be learning new things. Sometimes I like to work alone, and other times I like to work as part of the team. There are as many combinations and preferences as there are workers, and yours is one of them.

Realize of course that what you like may not actually fit in with what the employer has in mind, so unless you just couldn't stand to be something that might not be your first choice, temper your answer with the knowledge that most workplaces rely on teamwork and flexibility from their employees. Only you can decide if what they are presenting as a possibility is something that you could live with. As part of your consideration here you will want to think about how long you might have to live with it. Have they told you that things are changing and the described changes are more to your liking? How long will it take to make the changes? Can you hang on that long? Is this job just a gateway to greater possibilities within the company? What are those other opportunities? How long will it take to move into one? Can you wait that long? Is this a job you need for the moment, to earn some money while you look for the job you really want? How long does that take?

When I first went to work in the University environment, I took a job that I saw as a stepping stone. I had the whole scenario laid out perfectly. I'd take this junior accountant job to get my foot in the door. My research had shown that there were always jobs coming available that were more along the lines of my experience level and within six months I'd have one. Two years was long enough to spend there and then I would move into the ranks of upper management. Five years there and I'd be ready to be one of the top dogs. I had all the right experience and education. Everything was good with the economy. This was a no brainer. As it turned out, things didn't quite work out according to my little plan. I spent the next eight years applying for few opportunities, and never did budge out of that junior accountant job.

Best or Worst Boss

How do you deal with authority? That's not what they will ask directly, but it is what they are trying to find out when they ask a question like, "Can you describe your best/worst boss?" The message you convey with your answer should indicate that you can get along well with a wide variety of bosses. But here again, you need to be honest so that you don't end up working for someone whose style you just can't bear.

Good bosses are people who are constantly teaching, adding nuance and detail all the time, but who will let you fly solo when you know how to navigate the job. They will mentor you throughout your career. They will help you add to your skills without fear that you will surpass them.

You will find them supportive when you are right and instructional when you are not.

Not such good bosses are micro managerial, power crazed, possessive and will do anything to further their own career. They are not interested in what they can do for you, only what you can do for them and will dump you in a heartbeat if you make a mistake. OK, so I have an opinion.

I've had some lousy bosses, and some really lousy ones. All of them were a little different, and had their own way of being less than ideal people to work for. Let me caution you here that you should never identify one of these bosses by name, or by employer. You don't want word getting back to them. Or heaven forbid, the person interviewing you today actually knows one of these people.

Then again there have been people I would do anything for because they were such good bosses. These are the people you use as references. You can feel a little more confident in identifying these people. If they are as great as you think, they will have good reputations within their community and if the interviewer knows of their reputation, this can help you. Of course, your interviewer may have some reason to not care for your favorite boss and will see you as being guilty by association. Be prepared to explain what qualities make that person a good boss. They asked for your opinion, and this is it.

What Would You Change?

Part of your mission, should you decide to accept it, may be to fix something in the organization that is broken. If this is the case, it's very possible that you might be asked about what you would change first, or in the short term, to make the necessary corrections. You want to be careful with this one.

People say change is good, but change for the sake of change doesn't always work out too well. You need to answer so that they will know that you realize there are changes needed, but at the same time that you want to be sure that any changes you might make will be effective. Say something to the effect of, "I've gotten a brief look at the operation and have some ideas, but before making any major changes I'd like to get a closer look at things to see what the priorities are."

You need to look and ask questions. A clear understanding of what the desired result from the change is must be your first goal. From there you have to fully understand how things are currently done, and why that isn't working.

What ideas do others have? Could be that the guy who's been doing some job for twenty years has the perfect solution, but no one will listen. Or it may be that lots of things have been tried and didn't work. That's not to say that looking at the same solution with new eyes won't produce a better idea, but you may be able to weed out a couple of options and not waste time covering old ground.

Thought has to be given to what things could be done immediately and what might take some time to get going. And of course there are cost considerations. Are there viable solutions that are economical? Will it take a huge investment to right the ship? That's all for after you get the job, but you need to convey that message.

What Does Your Future Hold?

So often people want to ask, "Where do you plan to be in 5 or ten years?" They may be asking you that because they just want to know what you think you'll be doing in 5 or ten years. Or they might be asking to see if you've thought at all about a career path, or if you have any interest in a career. Maybe they just know they are supposed to ask that one, but aren't really sure why and couldn't think of a better one. Regardless of their reasons, there are a number of ways to answer this question.

The one thing you don't want to say is, "in 5 or ten years I'd like to have your job." That sounds like a lofty goal to you, but to the person on the other side of the question it sounds a little threatening. What they hear is, "I want your job, so look out!" Their reaction will be, "I can fix that by not hiring you!"

You want to leave it somewhat open ended so that they will see that you are flexible. You'll want to let them know that you are a team player, and that (at least to some extent) you want to do whatever helps the organization most. You want to be learning and growing so you're building the skills you have to offer. You want to try a number of things as your abilities and opportunity allow, so that you can get the broadest overview of how the company works. That puts you in a better position for long range advancement. Just don't say you want to suck the company dry by gathering knowledge and collecting a huge paycheck, then bolt to some other company, or start your own consulting business.

The person doing the interview understands that nothing stays the same. People change over time and so do their interests. The organization may have their own plans for you as well. Unless you are real familiar with the company or the job or the career track, you may very well not have any idea where the job you are interviewing for might lead. You might see it taking you one way when in actuality it opens many other avenues for you. If you really know exactly what you want to do, and have no leeway for straying from that course, then go ahead and say so. It's always best to be up front with the employer, and with yourself.

It's important to mention here, and to always keep in mind, that there is no point in saying something that you think they want to hear if it isn't really you. If you think they are looking for a hardnosed and decisive leader, but you are more easy going and group oriented, you put yourself on a path headed toward failure if you aren't just honest with them, and yourself. Sooner or later your lack of the qualities they were looking for will surface and you'll once again be on the prowl for a new job. To thine own self be true.

That leaves a lot of folks still scratching their heads as to an answer. If your plans are unclear, then your answer needs to be vague. Notice I say vague, but not unclear. You must convey a clear message to the interviewer, even if that message says you're not sure. Here are a couple of things to think about.

You'll want to indicate that whatever you will be doing, you expect to be doing a good job of it. Tell them you'd like to be completely fluent with the work at hand, and that you want to have established a good reputation within your work group, and the organization as a whole, for quality work. Suggest that you want to be open to learning the broader aspects of the work being done in the company in order that should advancement opportunities come available, you would be in a strong position to further your career. If you are talking to your immediate supervisor about this, they may not be thrilled to hear that you one day might leave, but you have qualified your answer by indicating that you want to stay long enough to learn everything and to do good work. No one is going to hold ambition against you. They might even think more of you than if you said "I'd like to have this job forever and never advance."

- These questions give an employer some idea as to how you will treat them.
- Think these answers out carefully.
- Listen to your answer. Would you take a chance and hire you?

Chapter 17
Excuse me?!

Over the years I have been asked some odd questions. Odd in that they didn't really pertain to the job or to the company or my experience, but more to me as a person. These were questions asked to more clearly define myself as an individual, and to see how well I could think on my feet.

The first time that happened to me it really caught me off guard. The question was "what is the last book you read?" There is no right or wrong answer; there is just whatever is the truth. You do have to come up with some kind of answer, or risk looking like a dumbo. What kind of person doesn't read? If you feel guilty about what you read, you can always say that you also read other things, but that's the last thing you read. Be prepared with something that sounds like a highly intellectual, or at least job related kind of book.

When you give the impression that you try to keep up what's going on in your line of work you give yourself a leg up over the "uninformed" competitors. Whether you are a doctor keeping up with the latest surgical techniques, a teacher on top of the latest learning theory or a plumber following the latest soldering trends, you demonstrate that you are professional, and really care about your work.

My response to the question the first time I heard it was that I was reading a book about sales presentations. I really was in the process of reading the book, but I hadn't turned a page in about three months.

Another question along these lines is, "if you didn't have to work, and had all the money you needed, what would you want to do?" Surely that is something we have all thought about, but we hardly expect to be asked by someone who wants to put us to work. Think fast. Tell them your dreams, or protect your greatest dreams and tell them smaller ones. I want to travel and to fund educational programs in the arts, but no one knows the details. And yes, I do have some very specific details. I'm just waiting for the time and money, but I'm not in any rush, especially since I don't have any money. But there are lots of other things I want to do that might be a little more readily accomplished.

There have been occasions when I sat in on an interview as one of the decision making panel, and I got bored by the questions. I felt sorry for the poor candidate who had to sit through all of that. Knowing what it's like to be the outsider looking in at the interview, and how stressful and, yes, boring it could be, I try to always be the one who asks the weird question. I'm not trying to make anyone squirm in their seat as they are caught off guard. I'm actually trying to help them relax a little by giving them a chance to answer a question that doesn't have career ramifications. I'm trying to show that I am interested in them as a human being. Trying to demonstrate that I value individuality. I'll ask something really broad that gives them plenty of room to define the question, and thus the answer, in their own way. It may very well be only marginally related to the job under discussion. It may be only tangentially related to the relevant industry. I just want to hear them think.

One of my coworkers, in hearing me describe this questioning technique as our organization was searching for a new employee, said to me, "I'm glad that you see all of this as your own little personal entertainment." That's not why I do this.

Some people don't have any individuality, and some can't think on their feet, and some have no personality, and for these, this sort of question can be horrifying. Honestly, for many jobs this kind of question is inconsequential, and maybe even unnecessary. But if I do happen to ask such a question, I get some startled looks sometimes. People will make the mistake of telling me they weren't prepared for such a question. Don't say that. Never. You have to always seem prepared for anything. A better response is, "that's a good question.." Then think fast.

After interviewing for a slot in a post-secondary social sciences education program, I was told by the search committee that they felt I didn't have any personality and would therefore not be a suitable recruit. I don't remember being horrified by any of the questions I was asked.

According to the law, there are some questions that shouldn't be asked. That's not to say that they won't be asked, but if they are, you don't have to answer them. But there is a right way and a wrong way to refuse to answer.

First, what kinds of questions are out of bounds? Generally speaking, anything that makes you uncomfortable because it is personal or has no relation to the job. You can't be asked about your age, or your marital status. Nor do you have to answer questions about gender, sexual orientation or political affiliation. Race, religion and ethnic background are also out of bounds as are questions about disabilities. Even some very innocent sounding questions may be on the borderline. If you are asked about your extracurricular activities, they may just be trying to find out how you relax or stimulate your mind. Or, they could be trying to figure out what other organizations you belong to that don't suit their sensibilities.

Most employers know these questions are taboo and probably are asking by honest mistake and not with the intention of discriminating. Sometimes you just get caught up in the conversation and curiosity gets the best of you and next thing you know you've asked what is a seemingly innocent question but none the less falls into some proscribed category of illicitness. In researching this topic however, I did read a very short blurb, written by an HR professional, giving good ideas to other HR people on how to properly phrase the question so you get the information you really want. ("30 Interview Questions You Can't Ask and 30 Sneaky, Legal Alternatives to Get The Same Info, HR World Editors, 12/26/2008, HRWorld website, www.hrworld.com). But if you get one of these questions, you can do one of several things. You can turn lemons into lemonade, ignore the question, or refuse to answer.

When a lemon like "how old are you?" comes at you, you can answer with something you would like them to know without actually answering the question. You might say, "I have a great deal of work experience and maturity." Or, "I am looking forward to a long career with this company." Either way, they know you are old, but you've given them two positive things to think about rather than the possibility that you're going to retire after a couple of years.

Similarly, you can ignore the question by changing the topic completely. Ask one of your questions, or make a statement about what you've seen so far or your own qualifications.

If you choose option three, politely state that answering such a question makes you uncomfortable because you don't see how it relates to the job. Don't stop to take a breath, just move the conversation along before they can give you any reason. You don't have to shout out that you refuse to answer or that you'll sue if they ask any more questions like that. You may risk losing the job, but do you really want to work for a company that operates outside the limits of the law?

And if you really think that you are the victim of discrimination by an employer, labor union or employment agency because of your race, color, sex, religion, national origin, age, or disability, you may file a charge of discrimination with the **U.S. Equal Employment Opportunity Commission**. To file a charge, contact an attorney who handles labor issues or contact your local EEOC office.

- **Expect the unexpected.**
- **Know when the line is crossed, and how to respond.**

Chapter 18
Do Like This

As a candidate there are sometimes ideas you want to stress, or at least make sure are raised in order to demonstrate your suitability. Things that might not be clearly spelled out on a resume. You have to really make an effort to get it into the conversation because you may not be directly asked that question, or even given a chance to say much on your own. You need to be conscious of the most important information you want to give the interviewers, and aware of whether or not you have done so. Be alert to every opportunity to interject something you want them to know.

In my family we had very orderly conversations where one person would speak and everyone else would listen. It was rude to interrupt, so you waited for a break in the speech and could then interject your commentary. Most of the rest of the world conducts conversation a little differently though, with more of a free for all of speaking. It took me a long time to come around to this way of conversing, and I probably missed a number of opportunities to say important things. Now, if I want to say something, I have no trouble jumping in. There is still, in my mind, a point at which this crosses over to rudeness, but when you have only one chance to get your message out, you need to speak when you can.

When you speak, be sure to enunciate clearly. I don't have a deep voice, but at times it can be very gravelly.

And unintelligible. I speak, and I hear, but no one else seems to. So in an interview situation, I make a point of speaking up, and clearly. Mumling iz a pr mnr o speech.

One thing that I have noticed is that if you hold your head up straight, not with your nose in the air, just straight, it's much easier to speak clearly. I'm sure there is a medical reason for this related to air flow or something. This posture also conveys an image of self confidence. As I walk about in my daily adventures, I often encounter people walking along and staring at the ground. I don't know if they are afraid to look up, or need some extra help with putting one foot in front of the other, but it says to me that they are not friendly, and not sure of themselves. I notice this because I always walk with my head up. Mainly so I can see what's going on around me.

Remember to be inclusive when you are speaking. When someone asks you a question, direct your answer toward that person, looking directly at them while answering, but also remember to give each person a glance. As you finish, return your gaze toward the asker and indicate that you are finished. They may wish to ask a follow up question. and you should hold your gaze long enough to determine whether your answer has been sufficient, or if you should add something, or even ask if that's what they were looking for. You can often tell by the look on their face. If they smile and nod, then they would seem to be satisfied.

Mind you now, when I say satisfied, they may not have liked your answer at all, or they make think you are the dumbest thing on the planet, but they are satisfied that you have provided an answer to the question, even if it is the wrong answer. Or they may be greatly enamored of your reply. If, on the other hand, they have some kind of glazed over, stupefied look on their face, then you might want to offer a follow-up answer. Ask them if you've answered their question or if you can provide some more information.

When you get nervous do you start babbling? Babbling is going on and on endlessly without purpose, as opposed to blathering which is more of a case of tongue twisties when sounds come out, but not in the formation of words. You obviously don't want to blather, but babbling is equally bad. It will convey the impression that you don't know when or how to end a thought or topic of conversation. But more importantly, babbling opens you up to the possibility that you will say too much, and at its worst, too much of the wrong thing.

There was a time when I was interviewing someone for a position as a skilled trades worker. His resume looked good- plenty of experience, and he had references. I was a little taken aback when he came in for the meeting. His shirt looked as if he'd spilled yesterday's lunch on it and he'd slept in it just to be sure the stain set. He hadn't shaved since that mishap, or perhaps even earlier.

Since it was a position as a tradesman, I was willing to let the beard go, and even the lunch stain and wrinkled shirt. Don't get me wrong. I'm not saying all plumber's show their crack or that all painters drink, just that in skilled trades positions workers often get dirty. I might not offer the same salary as I would if he were neat and clean, but I'm still keeping him in the running. Then he opened his mouth and something very wrong came out. He was talking about his history and he looks me right in the eye and says, "thank God I'm not in rehab." Whistles sounded, red lights flashed and I immediately understood the beard, the wrinkles and the stains. The guy had just told me he had some kind of substance abuse problem. We finished the interview, and he was cooked.

Being nervous is a very natural condition under the interviewers gaze, but it is also something that can ruin your performance. If the interviewer sits there and gets distracted by something you are doing because of your anxiety, they won't be listening to the brilliant commentary you are laying down about your value to their organization. Squirming in the chair, wringing your hands, shaking your legs and biting your nails are all good examples of outwardly visible signs of nervousness.

You may have your own idiosyncratic tics, habits or expressions. Be aware of what yours are, and when they are beginning so that you can put a stop to them before they get out of hand. I know that when I get nervous I feel my lips begin to quiver and my mouth forming into a frowny face. I hope that this is something that I feel much more than those I am addressing can see, but I've never really been sure. I do know that if I don't say, "gee, I'm nervous!" then my listeners won't say, "Gee, you seem nervous." If you don't mention it, they probably won't notice it.

My own experience tells me that being well prepared and well rehearsed is the best way to stave off nervousness. When I know what I want to say, and get past the initial jitters of meeting someone new, I do well. Other people may prefer to take a deep breath before they go into the meeting. In through the nose and out through the mouth, half a dozen times before you start. You don't want to overdo it though. Hyperventilating and passing out in the lobby doesn't make a very good impression on your prospective employer.

An age old means by which people relax involves the consumption of drugs or alcohol, but you definitely want to avoid this. You may think you are cool, but no one is going to miss the tell tale signs. Being drunk or stoned on the job is more than a bad idea.

- **Be sure to get your points across.**
- **With head up, be calm.**
- **Don't overdo it.**

Chapter 19
The Flip Side of Questions

Unless you are just desperate for a job and will take anything offered, you want to be sure that you will be happy in this job should you be chosen to fill it. Be prepared to ask questions, and don't be afraid to press a little for answers. It's your interview; it will be your job. Take control!

I've sometimes wondered if it seems rude to be taking notes while the other person is answering your question. The conclusion I've come to is that if you are really interested in the answer it won't hurt to write it down. You will demonstrate that your query was out of genuine interest. It will also assure you that the answer provided will be remembered much the way it was provided, rather than as you remember it an hour or so down the road when you can take notes outside the interview. You don't have to write down everything, but keep up with the important stuff.

Do your homework. You'll want to ask questions that are truly inquisitive, and questions that are designed to show that you already know a good bit about the organization, but still need some details. The interviewer will be impressed if you show that you have enough interest to do some research about the company. As an example, you might ask something like, "I see you have 12 plants in Eastern Nebraska, are there plans for further expansion?" Of course, you fill in the appropriate number and state.

You can tie similar questions to the product line, customer demographic, or any other pertinent aspect of the company's operation.

A good question to ask is always, "where do I fit on the organization chart?" You need to know who you report to, and who they report to. They may actually have a drawn out organizational chart to show you, or maybe they have a suggestion of where to look to find one. But they should be able to draw one out for you, or at least explain it, even if the company has no formal chart. You don't want to work in a place where there is no thought given to chain of command. That might sound like it would be very democratic if everyone was on the same level, and some organizations are very flat in their structure, but someone has to be in charge, and everyone has to know who. Kind of primitive, like a colony of apes, but that's how it's been done since we emerged from wherever.

It's always interesting to see how many levels of command separate you from the very top. I have had jobs where I was the top, where I was one step from the top, and where my boss's boss's boss was four Texas two steps away from the top. Sometimes it's good to be near the top because you are more likely to have people listen to you. But it can be nice near the bottom too, because you never get held responsible for things. Overall though, I recommend working your way up, or at least striving for that.

Along these same lines, it can be helpful to know how many employees there are in the company, and how spread out they are geographically. How many new names are you going to have to learn? How much of a cog in the wheel are you? How much competition will there be for advancement into how limited a pool of higher positions?

When you work for a small company, you have to be comfortable with the idea that you won't get an opportunity for advancement until somebody dies. Of course that doesn't only happen in small companies. In one of my good government jobs I realized that people like their good government jobs so much that they will stay there for thirty years. And all that while you are waiting for them to retire or perish so that slot might open up for you. Of course, in a big organization, there are lots of other people waiting in the wings along with you, and you may one day discover that you spent thirty years waiting for a slot that never came your way. I'd be mad as hell.

Generally speaking however, a large company will tend to offer more advancement opportunity in terms of the total number of openings available. You will probably also find that a large company offers more avenues of advancement, with positions in many fields of expertise. By that I mean that you will be able to gain experience in a number of different areas, if you choose, and move up along several possible lines of progression. In a small company, you may easily get pigeon holed, or there may only be one avenue for advancement available. There are too many scenarios here to discuss them all, so just think about all that when you are looking for a job.

People are sometimes reluctant to talk about benefits at the first interview. Seems they are afraid that bringing this up might send the wrong message- only interested in what the company can do for me. As I've said many times already, a job is supposed to be a win win situation. You help the company with their work and in turn they compensate you. Part of the compensation is the benefits package and you need to be aware of what is available before committing to the job. You might feel bad if they told you later that there is no health insurance. Or you might feel trapped if they told you later there was no paid vacation. They want you to be happy, so ask away.

Another query might be something like, "in filling this position, what exactly are you looking for in candidates?" That helps you in two ways. First, it tells you what strengths they see in you, and possibly gives you a clue into what your weaknesses might be in their eyes. But more importantly, it gives you an opportunity to recap your qualifications as you check off the list that's just been provided. You want to take every opportunity to show that your background fits with the job at hand, and why you are the best candidate.

Should you arrive at the interview without any questions, and state that when given the opportunity to ask, you will be seen as unprepared, unconcerned, and most importantly, as unworthy. I always make a list of things I want to know, even if some of them are kind of basic. When I say basic, don't go so basic that you are asking questions like, "So what does this company do?" That's too basic and you need to know that kind of information in advance. What I mean is, who does this position report to, how many people does this position supervise, what is the advancement potential, what are the limits of your autonomy?

If it's near the end of the interview, ask what the hiring process is. What is the next step in the process? What is the timeline they are looking at in filling the position? When would they want you to start? At this point you might hear the interviewer ask, "when would you be available to start work?" This may be a truly inquisitive question for planning purposes, or it may just be something to say. Keep in mind that the caveat is that these unspoken words apply: should you be chosen for the position. So, don't get all excited and blurt out, "I can start tomorrow!!!"

Whether you are currently working or not, it is a pretty rare person who can get all of their affairs in order overnight to start a new job on less than 24 hours notice. If you are not currently working, you can let them give you an idea as to how soon they really need you. You could say that you need a couple of days to get ready so you could start within a week, but add, "Unless you need me sooner." See what they say to that.

If you are currently working, you have to demonstrate your professionalism. You need to show them how you might treat them if and when you decide to leave their employ. It's customary to give at least two weeks' notice to an employer upon your departure, although some positions will require a longer time frame. Tell them that you feel an obligation to your current employer and that in all fairness you need to give them a (fill in the blank) notice. That may still leave your current employer in a bind if they can't fill your position in that time frame, but you have done your part to fulfill your obligation. Beyond that, it's not your problem, but you might not want to actually say that.

This whole line of questioning shows that you are planning ahead to fill the job. You may also hear something in their response that gives you a clue as to the strength of your candidacy. Answers like, "we're reviewing lots of candidate files and will be back in touch with the best," aren't very reassuring. But they don't necessarily mean you are out of the running.

You might be surprised by the range of answers that might sound good, but aren't any kind of sure thing. "We'd like to check your references." I've had people check my references before even interviewing me (which I think to be a poor practice), so saying they want to check them after the interview doesn't mean much. Maybe they will and maybe they won't. "I'd like to have you come back to talk to some other people." Unless you are the only one invited back, this could just narrow the odds for you.

Take the opportunity to ask for a clarification, or elaboration on something. While you have been talking and listening your mind has been whirring and new ideas have hopefully been popping up along the way. For example, if travel is involved in the position, you should find out if your expenses are reimbursed or if you have an expense account. A ten day trip overseas might be painful if you have to put it on your own Visa card and wait for the reimbursement.

Finally, if you really have no further questions, you can say that you had a list of questions, show them the list, and state that they've all been answered. They may then offer to have you call them if you should have other questions, or not. If not, ask if you may call them should you think of anything else. They'll say yes unless you are a real loser and you don't even have a snowball's chance in hell of getting the job. They may not take your call, but they will say yes.

- **Make a list of questions that you want to ask.**
- **Listen for opportunities to create other questions.**
- **Be sure to get the answers you need.**

Chapter 20
The All Important Issue of $$$

OK, so here's the question everyone wants the answer to, but everyone is a little reluctant to address. It's like the elephant in the room. Yes, it is a very important question. And yes, it can be a deal breaker. "So, how much does this job pay anyway?"

This is another homework question. Trying to wing it here can be disastrous. Let's step back a little to before the interview. OK, so you know this job is available. Maybe you heard about it from a friend, or maybe you saw it on line somewhere, or in the newspaper. Wherever. If you're lucky, the employer listed a salary. Maybe a salary range. This gives you a big leg up. You know right away if the job possibly pays enough to make you happy. Salary ranges can be tricky though because sometimes that's really the range they will offer to start, or, it may be the range available to you over the life of your career in that position. You need to know that, the difference can mean a lot. But it's a starting point.

If they didn't offer any guidelines, you need to find out what the job is worth in general. There are several websites that give guidance on salaries. Try www.payscale.com, www.salary.com or www.salary.nytimes.com. They can pinpoint it to the job title in your geographic area. But you gotta remember, these websites offer information based on statistics, and statistics are easily manipulated to say whatever the reader, or writer, wants them to say. You need to be able to compare the duties and responsibilities of the position you are looking at to the duties and responsibilities of the various titles you will find on these websites. Not all people with the title accountant, for example, do the same kind of work. Thus, their pay will not be the same. Some people with the title accountant are really chief financial officers bearing the full weight of the financial picture of their organization. Others with the same title may be data entry clerks. Different pay, same title.

I was once hired for a job and the Director of the organization told me to come up with my own title. He wanted something reflective of what I would be doing and since there was no established title that fit the diversified job I would have, I was allowed to develop my own title. I picked a title leaning toward the chief financial officer end of the scale, which the boss thought was well chosen. And I was paid at that level, but strangely enough, the work I was doing was much closer to the data entry end of the scale. Needless to say, I was not with that organization very long.

You can find out a lot of information on the above mentioned websites. Based on your education, how big the organization is, how many subordinates you will have, how much experience you have, the specific industry etc, you can get to a reasonable estimate of what the job is worth in the general market, and in the applicable geographic area. Of course, every employer has their own ideas, which may or may not concur with the general market. But it's a starting point. You'll know right away if the salary level is what you are looking for. Don't leave home without this info.

The best thing to do in an interview regarding the salary issue is to wait for the employer to raise it. They may ease into it with a question like, "are you comfortable with the posted salary rates for the position?" or they may be more blunt and say, "What salary do you expect to be paid?" Regardless of how they offer the question, it's in your best interest to fend them off with a non committal answer. You don't want to be the first to offer a dollar figure.

You can err in several ways by doing this. If you offer a high number, they will think you over value yourself, or are not in touch with the market value of your skills. If you offer a low number, they will again question your knowledge of yourself and the market, but add a question about your self confidence. They won't talk to you long if they think you will reject their offer as too low, and they know how much they can pay. And they won't take you seriously if you come in too low. They may think they can save a buck or so by bringing you in at a bargain basement salary, but in the long run, you will eventually realize your mistake and will either demand a raise, become bitter, or just leave, at which point they have to invest again in finding someone to do the job.

I worked in a place once where pay rates were based on aggression rather than any meaningful criteria. By that I mean that the people who most vehemently insisted on a higher salary were paid better than the people who had the most job related education and experience. Didn't have anything to do with glass ceilings, gender bias or any other form of discrimination. It was just the squeaky wheel getting the grease. When the other wheels on the vehicle found out about the salary discrepancy, there was a lot of hate and discontent, and the squeaky wheels soon left for oilier pastures.

So, deflect this question with an answer indicating that you understand their budgetary considerations, and that they are well aware of the value of your skills and the position in the general market, and that surely they have a fair and equitable plan in mind. End of answer. Let them chew on that.

At that point one of three things will happen. The subject will be changed without commitment. They will offer a number. They will press you for an answer.

If the subject is changed, it either means that they are ok with your answer and that they do have something in mind which they will discuss when they are confident that you are their person, or it means they are dismissing you as a candidate. You will know as the conversation progresses, or doesn't, which way they are leaning. When they know what they can offer, and you come across as being reasonable and confident in knowing that you have a certain value, they may very likely continue on the assumption that if everything else is in place to everyone's satisfaction, then the salary issue can be worked out. If they are dismissing you, the conversation will end quite quickly.

If they offer a number, you can play with the math a little. If it's a number you really like, ask them if they are offering you the job at that salary- ask for a commitment. If they back down, you have the upper hand because you know that they can offer that amount when the negotiation gets more intense later. If indeed they are offering you the job, don't jump in feet first quite yet. You may leave something on the table. Tell them it's very generous and that you are very interested but that you would like to consider it for a day or two and discuss it with your significant other or whoever. You can then come back and try to negotiate something higher or more studded with perks.

If they press you for an answer, then this is where the homework you've done, if you've been paying attention to me, is the rubber that meets the road. Don't just blurt out a number; you have to build to it. Indicate that you've done your homework. Let them know you know the value of your skills. Let them know you know what their competitors pay. Be confident and tell them what you're worth! And then you have to offer a number.

It's best here to offer a range, which still leaves you some wiggle room. The range has to be wide enough to give you that room, but not so wide as to be all inclusive. You don't want to say, "Oh, I was thinking between 50 and 100." If you want 50, say you were thinking something in the 50s. If you want 100, say you were thinking in the range of 100 to 110. Let them decide where in the range they can go, but don't sell yourself short. Don't take something that you won't be happy with or you'll be out there looking for a job again before you know it.

- **Know what the job is worth.**
- **Be confident of your abilities.**
- **Let them make the first move.**
- **Show no fear, or desperation.**

Chapter 21
Showing Up
And
Looking Good

Showing up is half the battle. I've heard this many times, in different forms, but the basic idea is that just showing up counts for a lot in whatever you are trying to do. It's no different with interviewing.

I have never heard of a person getting a job after not showing up for their interview. That's not to say that there are not cases where people have gotten jobs without having to go to an interview, but that's a different matter entirely, reserved for the realms of who you know, and how well you know them.

So, let's go back to the real world scenario of what happens with people like you and me. When I was trying to hire someone as an administrative assistant, I called one woman to schedule her interview and must have caught her quite by surprise. Mine was apparently not the only position she had applied for as her first statement to me was, "what company are you, and what position are we talking about?" That didn't give me a good feeling, but I just thought the situation was as described. We set up a time and she knew where the offices were so on the appointed day, at the specified time, I was eagerly awaiting her arrival. She was late. I finally realized that not only was she late, she just plain wasn't coming. No call, no email, no explanation. Maybe she got another job. It had been two or three days since I spoke with her. As I do put great value on my time, I wrote her off as a candidate ten minutes past our appointment.

But the story doesn't end there. Later in the afternoon she sent an email stating that she was very interested in the position and would like to be considered for an interview. I responded that we had scheduled an appointment for that morning, and thanked her for her interest. I don't know why I felt compelled to answer her at all. And I'm still not sure if she is just scatterbrained, or inept. I do know that I don't want to hire her.

When you are interviewing for a job, you need to be sure you look like you will represent the company well in that position. The appearance has to fit the role. So, if you are there to talk about a job as the groundskeeper, you don't need to wear a suit, but if you are there to talk about a senior executive position, you do wear a suit- a good one. That's what makes getting dressed so tricky sometimes- most jobs fit in between somewhere.

A lot of companies have more relaxed dress codes where even the president wears "business casual" every day. But it's hard to be sure sometimes, so it's best to err on the side of being a little overdressed. That way you have made an impression that you care about how you look and how others see you. You look professional. There is always the opportunity to tone it down later, after you get the job, but it's pretty hard to make a second first impression.

In management or executive positions, whether you are a man or woman, you'll want to wear a dark suit. Gray or blue are the colors of choice. Black is too powerful. Brown is unusual. Green is too much. It may be tempting to make a fashion statement, but go with a traditional style. Things got a little weird in the '70s. Another place to avoid a statement is in your selection of a shirt color, and tie. You want the interviewer to see you, not a shirt or tie. Wear a white shirt. Light blue is also acceptable. I liked to wear white to the first interview, and blue to any follow-ups. Personally, I didn't want them to think that all I had was one white shirt. With neckties you need to stay simple. Stripes or small patterns are OK. Red or blue. I am a shoe nut and will tell you that a wide range of shoes styles exist. Lace up shoes are preferred. You can wear loafers on casual Friday. The most important thing is to make sure that the shoes are freshly polished. Clean and shiny. Always wear socks. They should match your suit. The belt should match the shoe color, and also be polished. Boring maybe, but the standard and expected attire for job interviews of this sort.

Ladies, the uniform is similar for you. You can choose between a skirted suit or a suit with pants, but the color choices are again best kept to blue and gray. White shirt. Wear shoes with modest heels. You have more leeway with accessories and depending on the specific job and company, you may want to take advantage of that leeway.

Once again, to avoid flashiness, you will want to keep your jewelry to a minimum. I wear a watch and my wedding ring. Guys, this isn't really the time to show off your gold necklace, or bracelets. That pinky ring may look pretty good to you, but leave it home for once. Just today. Ladies, you too can wear a watch and wedding ring. But you can also wear a necklace or pin that isn't overpowering, a bracelet, and a single ring on your right hand. You don't want dozens of bangles and a ring on every finger. Not today.

This isn't the place for bright red lipstick and loud, erotic perfume ladies, and gents. A subtle color, or gloss on your lips will do. You still look great, and people will instantly know that you are looking for a job, not a date. And please, unless you are interviewing for a job in the adult film industry, keep your physical assets under wraps. You want people to see you as a person, not a set of legs or breasts.

Scents are a very touchy subject. You certainly want to be freshly bathed and to wear deodorant, but when you walk into the room your goal shouldn't be to knock anyone out. Some people are very sensitive to scents, or odors as they will often call them. Any hint of "odor" is unpleasant for them. Often this is because of some allergy. A group of women in the building where I currently work have an office which they have dubbed the "no stink zone." So for their sake, and yours, go easy on scented deodorant, soap and perfume. Please do not come in reeking of tobacco.

Everyone please brush your teeth! Don't try to substitute chewing gum for this as gnawing on a wad of gum during your meeting will surely go over like a lead balloon, even at the Wrigley Company. Ladies, your hair should be reined in and under control. Men, shave and comb your hair.

I always like to get a fresh haircut a day or two before an interview. It's kind of a ritual, but it leaves me with a good haircut so I know that won't be an issue. On weekends I wear my hair one way, but during the week, when I have to go to work, I push it around into a different style. You will want to go with that Monday through Friday style, and save your weekend look for the weekend.

When you wear a facial hair you tread a fine line. I'm addressing the men here. Thank you. If you have an established beard or moustache, and it's full and thick, it's obvious that this is part of you established appearance. On the other hand, if you are just starting one, you need to be very careful about keeping it neatly trimmed. Otherwise you will find yourself in the category of men who wear a beard because they just plain ole aren't shaving. It looks unkempt, and it's obvious. People will assume that you don't care, are stupid, or are just a slob.

Job titles are often misleading. It's pretty common knowledge that in the banking business everyone is a vice president because the title replaces a higher paycheck. It makes people feel good to have a big title. Same thing is true in higher education. Case in point is the title "manager." Sometimes the company will be kind enough to distinguish between a real manager and a working manager, but not always. You should always try to get a good job description before you go to an interview, that way you can be prepared.

I interviewed for a management position with a large retail home improvement company once. It was through a special program for ex military people. I'd heard someone talking about it and how they were learning about finance and marketing and sales and personnel management and so much more. Naturally, it sounded like a good opportunity. I was actually surprised to get an interview because I knew it was a very competitive market, especially in the hometown area of the company headquarters.

With suit and tie, and clipboard ready for note taking, I entered the building. It seemed like everyone there was a building contractor- all wearing golf shirts and khaki pants and work boots. I talked to the receptionist and she told me to have a seat.

When the director of the program came to get me, he too was wearing the contractor uniform. When we sat down he asked if I wanted to take off the coat and tie to be more comfortable. I saw this as a test, but I gave the wrong answer. He really wanted me to relax and take off the coat and tie while I was thinking I needed to stay professional and told him I was ok. This would be a working manager position, no suit and tie needed. Never did hear back from that dude. Many years later I interviewed with one of their major competitors and I remembered that experience. I wore khakis and a golf shirt with work shoes.

Never heard back from them either. The last time I was in that store I thought about that interview, and decided I was glad that I didn't get the job because I really wouldn't have been very good with it.

An even more outrageous example happened when I interviewed as a manager with a well known chain of breakfast restaurants. Same suit. Same result. The thing here was that they wanted me to cook the food. That was management. No suits need apply.

Of course, you can always go the opposite way and be underdressed, whether purposely or not. Right out of graduate school, I had an interview with a very large bank in a very large city. It was for some kind of marketing job- right up my alley education wise. I put on the suit and tie and talked to the head of human resources and a couple of days later she invited me to come back for a second meeting. This time with the Vice President for Marketing and a team of folks I'd be working with. Needless to say, I was very excited.

The interview was scheduled to begin mid morning and last until mid afternoon. It would also include a working lunch. I'd be meeting with some people individually, some in a group, eating with everyone and taking a tour of the bank. I didn't live near this big city and driving early enough to get there in time would have been pretty hard, so I flew. Even flying, I still had to get up at the crack of dawn and be on the flight right after the red eye. I was nervous all the way there and the gentle putt putt of the engine in this puddle jumper aircraft didn't help to ease my nerves.

The HR director greeted me and took me on the tour. She introduced me to a number of people who all got a chance to talk to me. At lunchtime, she introduced me to the VP and the whole group of us walked down the street a couple of blocks to the restaurant.

It seemed to me that during the interview the VP was directing his questions and conversation at everyone but me- it was a working meeting, but for employees only. Perhaps that was his way of getting the conversation started, or perhaps he was waiting for me to jump right in. When we got back to the bank, he disappeared back to his office without ever saying a word to me. I carried on the rest of the interview like I really had some sort of chance, but I knew. What I didn't know, and discovered with great horror finally when I was on my way home, was that the collars on my button down collar shirt were in fact unbuttoned. A minor detail perhaps, but apparently in the banking business, that akin to not being able to add.

- **Know the dress code.**
- **Understand what the job is.**
- **Know the dress code.**

Chapter 22
Um, Is This My Floor?

It may be that you find yourself out of your element. Wrong level of education. Wrong point in your career. Wrong social strata. Maybe just the wrong floor on the elevator and your clothing choices reflect that inconsistency. As an undergraduate I spent one summer working for a contractor doing research for the Justice Department. My job was probably lower than dirt on a totem pole, but one that was very necessary. That brings up an entirely different discussion on social injustice, but I'll save that for another day.

I had seen an ad in the newspaper- no internet job boards then- and wasn't sure what the job entailed but called and set up an interview. They were looking for college students to work on a summer research project. The work was technically called coding. It involved reading and then answering a series of questions about what you read. It was all multiple choice but required a lot of critical analysis.

The initial interview was in the contractor's office which was filled with PhD research scholars- a real think tank. Dark mahogany wood indicated that this was a prestigious firm, at least for the Ph.D. research scholars. Not so much for the coders who would spend their working hours in a large bullpen with folding tables, but comfy chairs. We were all always amazed at how one of coworkers could be sound asleep while sitting in his chair and holding his reading material in front of his face, seemingly hard at work.

The offices were on K Street in NW Washington DC, which at that time, and I believe currently, hosts a number of the powerbrokers and think tanks of Washington, DC. When they talk about "inside the beltway," this is where they mean. The men wear dark blue suits with starched white shirts. Women have a similar version of the power suit. The sidewalks are filled with people in these uniforms at lunchtime.

I got off the subway at the station closest to the office, on Connecticut Avenue. I was wearing a pair of pants that hadn't seen daylight in quite some time. I had on a white shirt, but it was seriously lacking on starch. My necktie was brown. I remember that, but not why in the world I would ever have bought a brown necktie. I must have borrowed it from a roommate. It was wide, as was the fashion of the day. No jacket. To this day whenever I see college students in church with their semi formal, mismatched, rugged looking outfit I have to cringe. Having since become accustomed to wearing Italian loafers, I complete my embarrassment by saying that I think I might have worn Keds that day.

It was a windy day, as it often is in the concrete canyons of cities around the world. How do I remember all of this you might ask? Well, for one thing I have a good memory, but also because my trip to this interview had a profound impact on me. It was the heyday of the "me" generation, the Reagan Whitehouse, and here I am on power street USA. Dressed like a clown. I can't forget how it felt to be looked at by others. What I really remember was that I was just a tad late for my appointment, something else I strongly recommend against, so I was trotting down the crowded sidewalk.

I've always heard that seeing a man running through the streets always arouses suspicion- bank robber, pickpocket, and purse-snatcher. It's different if you're in running clothes, but then people stare at you like your some kind of nut. The combination of the wind and the trotting made the brown tie fly over my shoulder. I repeatedly grabbed it and flipped it back, only to have it fly off again. I tried slowing down. I tried holding it. Didn't matter, the thing just had a mind of its own. I very vividly remember a young woman looking at me with a horrified expression. Damn, she won't be going out with me!

It didn't seem too odd to me as I ran down the street that I was wearing sunglasses- prescription. Bright sunny day. When I got to the office however, the sunglasses became their own issue. I see about as well as a bat with broken radar, so I have to wear spectacles. I've always been a little rough with my glasses, so it was of no surprise to me that I had broken my good pair. I was wearing the sunglasses until I could get a new pair. Try to picture that on Powerstreet, inside the office building of a respectable organization. Not cool. But you know what? I got that job, and I wore the sunglasses all summer.

Toward the end of summer, the project was coming to a close and I was looking for another job. I had seen an opportunity with another contractor doing some similar work for the Justice Department. I sent in a resume, or what there was of one at that point, and waited to hear. Let me remind you that back in those days we didn't have Macs and PCs, we had typewriters. If you were lucky you had an electric one, maybe even the top of the line IBM Selectric III with a correction feature. Otherwise there was white out, or even trying to erase the wrong with a pencil eraser. Try to imagine the mess that might make in a resume produced by a sleep deprived college student.

I advise strongly against this, but I used the bullpen phone number at work as my contact number. I don't remember who answered that call, but it's a little hard to talk to someone to set up an interview in that environment. The woman wanted to talk to me that afternoon, 5 PM. I told her I wasn't really dressed for an interview-jeans, no socks, maybe a belt. She said it was ok. As it turned out, I was dressed perfectly for the job, and I got it.

- **Know what the job calls for.**
- **Dress the part.**
- **Always look your best, accordingly.**

Chapter 23
Travel Light

In discussing what to bring to the meeting, one normally thinks of things like a copy of your resume, in case someone needs one or so you can refer to it; a notepad to write down the answers to your many questions and the names of people you meet or just some good old info you pick up; the proper attire; and a smile. But I've noticed that some people, for a variety of reasons, like to bring other things with them.

If you are a graphic designer, writer, artist or architect, it might be a good idea to bring a portfolio of your work. That is definitely work related and would be welcomed at an interview. What I'm talking about is more things like, well, your mother. Or special friend. You know, boyfriend, girlfriend, hamster. You laugh.

I did once take my sister to the same city I was interviewing in, but it was an historical city on the east coast and she wanted to do some sightseeing while I was interviewing. That's a far cry from bringing someone into the HR office with you, or to the reception area. Sure, you're nervous and a friendly face can provide comfort, but unless you work strictly as a team with this person or thing, don't bring it.

In these times it's an absolute necessity to pull out all the stops and to use every resource available to help you land a job, but there comes a point in the process where it all rests on your shoulders. It's all you- your words, your actions that will make the impression on the interviewers. We've already talked about how someone else might provide a connection or a reference or throw some weight around for you, but if you make a fool of yourself in the interview, it's all you. Not to mention that you will probably lose the cooperation of that "friend" in the future.

I conducted a job search for physical plant maintenance workers once. I remember seeing a car in the parking lot with an older couple in the car and remarking to myself, "I wonder what they are doing here?" I was a little surprised to see the man come through the door for an interview, but he left his wife in the car and never mentioned her. On the other hand, I remember a time when my company was interviewing for recruiters in a large city. One woman arrived late, brought her boyfriend into the office with her, and then insisted that they had to leave early so he could pay some bills. Needless to say, she didn't get any further consideration.

Of course, that significant other may have considerable influence in your decision to take the job. Maybe they will tell you how much money you need to make, or what kind of company car you need to get, or whether they are willing to relocate. But they can give you a list of questions and specifications to take to the interview. What signal does it send to a potential employer if your wife comes in asking what holidays you get off, before you even have the job? Who makes decisions in your home? How good a decision maker are you? What are your priorities in life? You get the picture.

You remember the hamster I mentioned? That didn't really happen, but people certainly bring other things with them, including pets. And children. Sure, there are times when it's tough to find a baby sitter or daycare or whatever, but you have to work around things like that. The assumption is that if you arrive with some distraction, or some really odd thing, then you will repeat that behavior while you are working there. It's like wearing tennis shoes to an executive level interview. Unless your foot is broken, the shoes signal an anomalous thought pattern that will prove to be out of sync with your job duties and performance.

- **Show up alone.**
- **Bring only job related items.**
- **Save your individuality for outside the workplace.**

Chapter 24
Into the Fire

And so, almost finally, we come to the point where you actually get to the interview itself. All this time you've been preparing and planning, but now comes the moment of truth! The very most important thing, as a final hurdle before you jump into the fire, is to be on time. If you can't get to the interview on time, you will be late for work too. At least that is the assumption the interviewer will make.

I get a little bit carried away with this sometimes, but give yourself plenty of time to get there. Know how long it takes to get there, and allow a little extra for things like heavy traffic, detours, bad weather, etc. I would sometimes leave two hours early for a meeting I knew would only take an hour to get to. Just to be safe.

Of course, to know how long it takes to get there means you first have to know exactly where you are going. The Megalith Office Complex downtown isn't enough of an address to easily and quickly find the place you want to be. People will not mind giving you good directions when you set up your interview. They don't necessarily expect you to know where they are. Check out their address on MapQuest and print out the map and directions. These websites aren't always exactly right, so again, leave some time for details.

Find out in advance what the parking situation is. How far away is the parking? You may be able to park at ground level right at the company's front door, or you may have to find on street parking in a crowded area of town which means you'll have to factor in some searching time as well as some walking time. Do you have to pay? If so, you need to make sure you have enough money to cover the cost. A quarter in a parking meter at the curb may be sufficient, or it may be more like ten bucks to park in a downtown parking deck.

In what kind of building does your destination lie? If the company has its own private building, it shouldn't be too hard to find a receptionist, or someone to ask for directions to the person you are to meet with. To find a suite of offices on the eighty third floor of the Empire State Building you may need to first find the front desk to ask which elevator to take. The one that stops at each of the first thirty floors is not it, and neither is the one that starts at thirty one. You want the express to seventy five, and then switch to the local to the eighty third. Don't quote me on that. It's been a long time since I rode the elevators in the Empire State Building and I don't want you to blame me if you're late for that one.

On time, you've found your destination and you are ready to walk through the door. Back up one second. Take a look at yourself. Are you all put together? If I'd done this at the bank, my buttons would have been buttoned and now I'd be president of some huge bank. On second thought, right now that might not be such a good thing. Look in a mirror. Hair neat? Check. Smile pretty? Check. Finished dressing? Check. Use the restroom facilities if necessary. I always felt like I had to do this at least twice. Now, take a deep breath, tell yourself you can do it and walk through the door. Remember, this is not a confrontational meeting. They are not trying to be mean to you. They want to see if you meet their needs, and you want to see if they meet yours. Relax.

You'll be greeted by someone, perhaps a receptionist. Smile, introduce yourself and state your reason for being there. Say, "I am Superman or Wonderwoman, or whatever your name is, and I have an appointment with so and so at such and such a time." And the agony is prolonged while this kind person locates the one you want to speak with. "Have a seat, would you like something to drink?" they ask. This is not the time to lose your cool and say, "double scotch straight up." No, this is where you take a seat and say, "no thank you, I'm fine." You may be thirsty. Your mouth and throat may be as arid as the Sahara, but don't take the drink.

And here is why. When your person arrives to welcome you, you'll have this drink like an albatross. What are you gonna do with it? You don't want to take it with you because you don't want to be busy drinking your drink during your interview. You could just leave it there, making a ring on some table, leaving the receptionist to clean it up. You could toss it in the trash, which appears wasteful, or you could suck it down in a huge gulp and then toss it so as to not look wasteful. Whatever you do with it, you still have a cold and damp hand from holding the thing.

And you're gonna have to go to the restroom that much sooner.

When you go to greet the person, the proper thing to do is smile, introduce yourself, and shake hands. Be sure that you have paid at least some attention to the grooming of your hands. They should be clean at the very least. You don't want a cloud of dust rising when you shake someone's hand, nor do you want them to pull their own hand back to find it covered with grease. Nails should be trimmed, and clean. If you are a nail biter, try to go easy on them for a couple of days prior to your interview, and then maybe file them a little. You can bite your nubs after you get the job. If you are on the other end of the spectrum and keep your nails long, remember that you have to be able to use those fingers to do work so the nails can't interfere. Keep the polish tone down as well.

You'll know from experience how your hands react to the pressure of going into a stressful situation. Do they stay dry, or do they get clammy, or even real sweaty? There is a little trick you can do to solve any of this. As you approach the person, let your right hand kinda slide across your right leg. If you're a sweaty handed person, you may need a little more pressure than just a light swipe, but the idea is to dry your hand on your clothes and then shake hands. You need to practice this a little to be sure you do it in a real subtle way. Don't be real obvious.

The proper handshake, including a dry hand, can be more difficult than you might imagine. There are issues of pressure, duration and how many pumps? This isn't the place for the secret fraternity handshake or anything you learned at the gym or on the streets. Just a simple, traditional handshake. Extend your right hand, fingers together, thumb separated and sticking up. Interlock hands with the other person so that the vee created by your index finger and thumb is snuggling in the corresponding vee of the other persons hand, and your fingers and thumb wrap around their fingers.

Squeeze enough to let them know you are there. There is nothing worse than the dead fish grip in which you don't exert any pressure. However, the crusher grip isn't far behind. When you get the dead fish, your first instinct is to get it out of your hand ASAP. The crusher on the other hand, may be inescapable. You don't want to hurt the person, just say hello. I remember shaking hands with a guy once, under forgotten circumstances, where we had a crushing contest. After about 10 seconds we looked at each other and he asked me why I was gripping so hard. I replied, "You're the one who started squeezing!"

Handshaking should be natural, but it can be troublesome. I have gone to shake hands with people and actually missed the interlock, getting fingers incorrectly entangled. That's bad. Or I've gone to grip someone's hand and they just grab my fingers which leaves me unable to grip anything. In an interview setting, shaking hands is a welcoming greeting, not a power struggle for supremacy. Later on, after you get the job, you will want to know all of the hand shaking tricks that will give you the upper hand, so to speak, in the constant life and death struggle for the survival of the fittest in the business and political world.

You've made it through so far with the resume, the clothes, the hair and hopefully the handshake. Now its time to open the mouth and display your mind. And in doing so you will reveal a great deal about yourself as a person. How you interact is a huge opportunity for success or failure.

Everyone has a personality. I like to think that they are all good, just different. But, it's very easy to see that these differences mean that some personalities are better suited to certain work than others. Al Capone had certain powers of persuasion, but he wasn't what you'd call sales rep material.

There were numerous times in my interviewing career when I thought to myself that I could be what I thought they wanted for the job for an hour or so during an interview. And during that hour I would do my best to be outgoing, serious, professional, funny, sophisticated, down to earth or exhibit some such other trait. I almost always thought that I pulled it off pretty well. What only began to occur to me after a number of these meetings was that if I passed the test for the hour long interview, and that was the personality that the employer wanted, then somehow I was gonna have to be that way that first day when I showed up for work. And stay that way for however many years I stayed in that job. Trust me, you don't want to have to do that.

You are who and what you are. There are many things you can change if you really want to. Plastic surgery can work wonders with big noses, saggy eyes, chinless faces and bad smiles. Speech coaches can help you to lose a strong accent and to choose polished words. Acting classes might help with your public presentation. If you want to fit in with polite society you can take etiquette classes. And, you'll have no problem finding scholars and teachers who will tell you how and what to think.

But how plastic do you want to be? The real question here is who should you be to feel comfortable with yourself? That question takes us way off topic here so I won't delve too deeply into that thought. The main thing is to be you. Whatever that self is. When you feel good about yourself, comfortable in your own skin, it will be a lot easier to be relaxed. You won't be worried in the back of your mind that you are not sounding erudite enough. Or that you are laughing at the right time. Or expressing the proper opinions.

If you get a job under such false pretenses you will eventually begin to be uncomfortable. Or you may get caught in your lie. I'm not sure that you can get fired for faking your personality, but there are social consequences that can make life at work difficult.

Getting a good job certainly means putting out a lot of extra effort, but not in the area of being something you are not. You may need a job badly. And you can tell yourself that even if the job sucks, it will pay the bills and you can fake it until you find another one. But finding that next job may take longer than you think.

I went to what I thought was a stepping stone job once. It was ok, but it was a little too heavily concentrated in an area that I didn't love, and wasn't really well suited too. I was better suited to something a little higher up the totem pole. But this got me in the door, and paid the bills. I figured six months to a year and I'd be moving up. And up again not long after that. Damnedest thing though. Despite my best efforts, those six months turned into multiple years. Finally, I moved to the head of the class.

But having to fake it for that long can get to be miserable. Soon you find yourself hating your job. Dreading each day. Your performance can slip. Your attitude may need adjustment. You may even start drinking and. Hold it. That may be an extreme, and certainly wasn't my own situation, but you get the picture. You gotta like your job to be happy. Be yourself. Either they like you or they don't.

- **Know where you are going.**
- **Good handshake, friendly smile.**
- **Be yourself.**

Chapter 25
Play Nice

You have to walk a tightrope in terms of how you interact with each person. Of utmost importance is to be polite and receptive. As you are introduced, smile, shake hands and say, "nice to meet you," or just plain old "hello." Be sure to make eye contact, and hold it during the introduction. Just don't stare. And don't close your eyes when you talk to people. Giving the impression that you are sleeping during your interview is certainly a bad signal to send.

As you talk, and listen, be attentive. You could really pick up on some good information about the job or the company or the people. Something you see or hear might spark an additional thought. Sit, or stand, straight. Good posture says you care about yourself, which translates to you'll probably care about your job and the company you work for. It also says you are not lazy. That's important information for the employer, and they will pick up on it.

After a long day of travel and interviews I found myself back in the HR manager's office waiting for some next step. I was dog tired. And I was reclining in the chair. That was early in my career and I didn't pick up on the idea that her asking if I was tired wasn't out of concern for my well being. Rather, it was a commentary on my poor posture. Right. Didn't get that job.

You shouldn't have to think about this too much, but you should always have an appropriate expression on your face. That would normally be attentiveness, friendliness, agreement or inquisitiveness. When you see someone with a blank stare on their face you have to wonder where that persons mind is. And you are unlikely to think that it is all present in their head. Laughing at the wrong time can also send the wrong message. Think about what it says about your sense of humor. Do you laugh at things normally considered to be funny? Are you a morbid sicko? A smile can often indicate agreement, or a sense of understanding so such an expression can have many appropriate applications. But again, only at the proper times.

If you want to indicate that you are interested in the conversation, in addition to your expression you can use several other bits of body language. Lean in, toward the speaker, or the person you are addressing. That says you want to get closer. To connect. To hear. Because you are saying you fit in.

I told you to sit yup straight, just like mama did, but if you sit stiff as a board and don't move you come off like a robot. You can shift your weight around occasionally. Don't be noisy about it though. If you sit on a leather couch, squirming around makes a lot of noise. Put your arm or elbow alternately on the left and right arm of the chair you're in. Lean in, as above. Sit up. Speak with emotion, not in a monotone voice, and be demonstrative with your hands. You don't want to be flailing wildly, but a little movement of hands, wrists and forearms is ok.

Even if you are telling a really good story and get really excited, don't jump up out of the chair.

You want to be friendly and polite. But don't overdo it. Be sure that when you are speaking, you are loud enough that you can be heard, but not blowing out everyone's eardrums. Some people speak very loudly. I don't know if it because they just have a loud voice, they don't know they are doing it, or they just don't give a damn that everyone around them hears their business, and gets annoyed. It's the last possibility that interviewers will most likely interpret an overly loud voice to signify. It's ok to be exuberant sometimes, but sharing secrets with strangers has potential dangers. Especially if you work in a highly competitive field. Like espionage.

The other thing you need to think about is exactly how much you say. When you answer a question, you want to say something more than yes or no. You need to explain things, or make them interesting. However, you need to be careful not to say too much. You don't have to look at this process as adversarial. The interviewers aren't looking to trip you up. But you do want to be sure that everything you say is positive and sheds a complimentary light on yourself.

One thing to be on guard about is displaying your reaction to the people you are meeting. Maybe you don't like them. Are they just not like you? Too stiff? Too loose? Maybe they are hideously ugly, although beauty is in the eye of the beholder. Would you be happy working with these people? And here is the hard part of the tightrope walk. You don't have to change yourself to be like them, but do not do or say anything to make them think that you have anything other than the highest regard for them. You might not want the job, but you also don't want to burn a bridge. After you leave you can decide you couldn't work there. You can spit and wash your hands endlessly and shiver with that creeped out kind of chill. But that's after.

Now, bring on the questions!

- **Be friendly and polite.**
- **Be a little expressive, not a bump on a log.**
- **Most of all, be yourself.**

Chapter 26
Follow Up

All good things must come to an end, and so is it with your interview. How you handle the finishing moments and the follow up has just as much impact on the result as how well you perform during the interview.

When it's over, it's over, and you have to be able to recognize that moment. If you have asked all of your questions, and the interviewers seem to be finished with theirs, then that's it. Do not let it go beyond that or you run the risk of looking socially inept, and indecisive. It's ok for the interviewers to look indecisive, but not you. As I said, it's your interview, if you want the job you have to take control.

Start to gather your things and get ready to leave. If they are not finished, they will let you know. Stand up, and thank them for their time in speaking with you. State very clearly that you are very interested in the position and that you are well qualified. You can then shake hands with each person and leave. There may be a little bit of chit chat that they initiate regarding how nice it was to meet you and when you will hear from them. Be attentive and polite, but do leave.

Here is where you can do some valuable homework. As soon as you can, find a place to sit down and make some notes for yourself. Write down any important information you need to about the people, the company, the job and your impressions and thoughts. You are doing this for two reasons. First, you want some notes to refer to so you can mull over the merits of accepting an offer, what salary you think the job is worth, how you might rearrange the office, and so you can talk again about the job should you have further questions or be invited back for a follow-up interview. Second, you are keeping notes for learning about interviewing.

How did it go? Were you nervous? Could they tell? Did you have good answers to their questions? Were there any trick questions, or questions you weren't prepared for? Did you have good questions for them? Did you speak clearly? Was there good eye contact? Did you do or say anything stupid? How did they receive you? Any weird reactions?

Who were the people? Job titles? How does the job interact with these people? Did you like them? Did they like you? Would you like working there? What were the physical environs like? Did the offices look professional? Was it clean? Were they legit?

This kind of information fades fast from the memory so you need to write it down quickly. This may also help you to think of any follow up questions you might not have thought of during the interview. Depending on what they are, they can be addressed during a follow up interview, or in a call or email to one of the interviewers. Don't hesitate to ask questions- you will be regarded as sincere.

Momma always told you to say please and thank you and the interview process is no different. When you get home, or back to your office, or to the nearest computer, send each of the interviewers an email. You should have either gotten their business card during the interview, or you can look them up on the internet. In the off chance that you can't find them on the corporate website, or the company doesn't have a web presence, you can either call the office and speak to the secretary or receptionist to get that info, or you can send a note via snail mail. In any case, what you need to say is that you enjoyed meeting them and you are grateful for the time they spent with you.

I used to actually send a letter via the United States Postal Service. This is much more formal, and seems more respectful. Today however, it seems that email is a very acceptable format for this letter. I decided that one day when I had an interview where a decision would be made very quickly and unless I hand delivered the letter it would not get to the recipients, the decision makers, in time. I emailed, and have done so ever since.

Here is your opportunity to once again stress your strengths and compatibility with the position. Offer to address any further questions they might have and state that you are looking forward to seeing them again and working with them. Don't make it too long, email is intended to be short. One paragraph, two at most, will get the message across. What you are saying is, I'm professional, I'm interested, I'm qualified and I'm confident so hire me!

I have always done this, and was certain that it was a common practice, but in my various experiences on the hiring side of the table, I have been amazed when people did not follow up. It is important to send this message, EVEN IF YOU HAVE DECIDED YOU DON"T WANT THE JOB, because you do not want to burn any bridges in your job search. There is an old saying stating be nice to everyone you meet on the way up because you may see them again on the way down. What that translates to is that as you climb the ladder of success, you need to be nice to everyone. One day you will reach the top of your ladder and be king of the hill, but as is the nature of the game, there will be those who aspire to that position. As your glory days fade, some of those who you climbed over to get to the top will be rising themselves, and may step onto your shoulders. Will they do so with kid gloves, or hobnailed boots? One day, sometime in the future, you may meet these individuals you have just interviewed with again. Perhaps in another company, or perhaps in another job search. If they remember you well, you'll be much better off.

What I have described above is the bare minimum of what you might do as follow-up. How you proceed from here depends on how much you want the job. Are you desperate for work? Is this absolutely the best job you've ever seen and you can't stand the thought of not getting it? If either of these scenarios fit your situation, you'd better be prepared to do some more follow up,

The point of all this is that if you have a connection, even it's tenuous, use it. Here's where the benefits of all that networking you are supposed to be doing come into play. Remember, that's another book to read. If you are like me, you may not have wanted to bother people with this sort of thing before. Uncomfortable asking for favors. Get over it! Just be sure that the person you ask the favor of is in good standing with the person you are trying to get to. If you ask a known twit to recommend you, you too will be seen as a twit right off the bat. And once you've asked for the favor, never let them down.

Of course, this doesn't always work out the way you'd like. Your connection's connection may not be as strong as you would like. It could be that the person you seek help from is either not able, or willing, to provide any help, but doesn't want to say that to your face. You may never know who did how much for you.

I worked on a public service committee and asked the chairman to speak to one of the board members about a job opportunity available in his organization. I was no longer active on the committee and didn't really have direct access to the man, so I asked for the intermediary help. "Of course I'll talk to him," was the reply. Never did hear a word from either of them again, even though I was super qualified for that job. Maybe when you aren't fresh in someone's mind they decide they can't help. My thought is that it depends on the person. You just never know. But what's the harm in asking? So do it!

- Know when the party is over and it's time to leave.
- Take some notes to keep thoughts fresh.
- Send your thank you notes.
- Pull out all the stops you can.

Chapter 27
And Now We Wait

In some ways, this may actually be the hardest part- waiting for the results of all your effort. Hopefully, the employer will quickly give you a call and offer you the job. After a second interview for what seemed like a pretty damn good job, I was walking down the sidewalk, back to my car, when my cell phone rang. It was the boss man of the organization I'd just been meeting with. He offered me the job as well as the sun and moon. I hadn't even been out of his office for ten minutes!

But sometimes you'll have to wait longer. Hopefully with the same results. I waited weeks, and made several calls to the employer for what I knew would be the greatest job ever. They told me to hang in there. It would be worth my time. Since I didn't have anything else going on at the time, I waited. And waited. By the time they finally offered me the job, I was so tired of waiting that it just seemed like a huge anticlimax. But I loved that job! Most of it anyway.

And sometimes, you wait, and wait, and wait, but nothing happens. For many years I figured it was my duty to wait. If they wanted me, they would say so. Then I got tired of always waiting. And you shouldn't wait and wait. Call. Ask the status.

A short call to touch base and ask what's going on could very well be seen as just the enthusiasm the employer is looking for and enough to tilt things in your favor. But when they never call back, or won't answer your calls of inquiry, it gets pretty clear that you may not have made the cut. And you will find that often times you will not ever hear a peep from a potential employer, even after they have made some sort of investment of time in you.

How many times has someone said, "I'll call you" only to never be heard from again? Too many to count. I realize that people are busy, and I've done it myself in the past. You say to yourself, "I'm too busy to call all these rejects back, they'll get the picture." Karma is real!

As just one example that stands out in my mind, many years ago I applied for a position with a small private company in a large Southern city. I was responding to a newspaper ad calling for applicants. As I expected, I was granted an interview, at the end of which the HR person told me in no uncertain terms that I would be hearing from her within several days. That was Wednesday, and I have this weird aversion to finding out bad news just before a weekend so I thought nothing of it when Friday came and went with no word. When Monday also passed, I decided I would call on Tuesday. No decision yet, they hoped to make one today. Another call Thursday and no answer. On Friday I would normally have taken the bad news for the weekend concept into consideration, but decided I just wanted to know.

When I called Friday, I was told that a decision had been made on Tuesday, and I didn't get the job. Just because I wasn't selected I didn't want to be rude (never burn bridges), but I did expect some courtesy, so I asked why they hadn't called to tell me that. They said they did not want to disappoint me. I guess they figured that if they didn't say anything then I'd forget I was looking for a new job and had interviewed with them. Everyone wants to be the good guy, but sometimes you have to say no. It doesn't get any easier by delaying it. Anyway, I may be old fashioned, and no one ever said business had to be polite, but seems to me that everything you do in your job, whether as job seeker or someone seeking to fill a job, represents who you are.

It also turned out that they had concluded that I lived too far away from the office. It wasn't like I was on call or anything; I just had to show up at my regular time. I wasn't on the clock while commuting, so why should they care where I lived? I could have moved closer. They didn't ask me about that. Or maybe I like to drive in traffic for hours on end. But you'll find that the people doing the hiring will often come to conclusions about you based on their own misguided and uninformed assumptions. You know, the old ass u me thing. Aw hell, I wouldn't have wanted to work with those rude people anyhow.

Just remember this- while you are waiting to hear about one job, do not fail to apply for any others you encounter that are of interest. The more irons you have in the fire, the more likely you are to strike pay dirt. Maybe you'll even be in the enviable position of having to decide between multiple offers, in which case you can look in the mirror and say, "Ain't I wonderful?!"

You can't control what the employer does. There will be jobs for which you are well qualified, but you won't get an interview. Don't get your panties in a wad. There will be other jobs, and you will get the opportunity to interview. Once you have this small toehold, remember the things I've described in this little book, follow my advice, do your best and the next thing you know you'll be strutting down easy street . Best of luck in your search for fruitful employment.

- **Sometimes you have to wait.**
- **Don't be afraid to ask for a status report during the waiting period.**
- **Show your interest.**

Epilogue

You hear about big business deals being sealed on the golf course all the time. I've never seen that, but then, I don't play golf. But I did once have an interview at the lake that involved a jet ski. Well, it wasn't really a formal interview, but it was an encounter with a rich guy who owned a business and could have given me a job. He was my mother in law's sister in law's cousin. Something like that. Real close.

He brought his new boat to visit us at the lake house. The damn thing was all engine, and a lot of noise. Too big for our lake- maybe good for one of the Great Lakes. His son had followed him over on their new jet ski. This was a long time ago, before they were called personal watercraft. You had to stand up on the thing to ride it. These are popular with trick riders I think.

We were all visiting on the dock, and Mr. Rich and I were talking and he tells me to go for a ride on the jet ski- it'll be fun. I love boats and the lake, but up until then, I've never ridden a jet ski before. OK. I've been scuba diving and skydiving, I'll try this. Unless you are really good and can jump on the thing standing up from the dock and hit it full throttle, you have to start out by crawling onto the thing, which is quite wobbly, and then start out and kind of pull yourself up to a standing position. I don't mind being wet, but I wasn't expecting to drink the whole lake.

I start out, slow, and speed up, pulling as hard as I can to get up. At this point I think a reasonable description of my physical self will help you see what's happening here- picture an apple with toothpick arms. I'm pulling and pulling, but can't get myself up out of the water while the Jet Ski is hurtling forward through the water. I'm eating water while this sucker drags me around. It didn't take long for me to get bored with this, so I swung back by the dock and Mr. Rich calls out that it's more fun if you stand up. I wave, let myself be dragged around for another minute or two and then pull up alongside the dock and slide off into the water.

I thought about staying under, and maybe swimming away, but instead I came up and climbed up onto the dock to dry off. Mr. Rich then said he had to go, and told his son to take the boat. The boat roars off, and Mr. Rich leaps onto the Jet Ski from the dock and disappears, never to be heard from again. I laugh about that now and if you can picture the scene you would laugh too, but at the time I felt really stupid. I still feel like an apple with toothpick arms. The point is though, that you are being evaluated with everything you do, and interviews take all kinds of forms. You have to have your game on in the conference room, in the parking lot, the golf course, and even on the damn Jet Ski.

www.ingramcontent.com/pod-product-compliance
Lightning Source LLC
Chambersburg PA
CBHW032020170526
45157CB00002B/781